SHARKS

SHARKS

Ancient Predators in a Modern Sea

Salvador Jorgensen

FIREFLY BOOKS

A FIREFLY BOOK

Published by Firefly Books Ltd. 2013

First printing

Publisher Cataloging-in-Publication Data (U.S.)
Jorgensen, Salvador.
Sharks : ancient predators in a modern sea / Salvador Jorgensen.
[256] p. : col. photos. ; cm.
Includes bibliographical references and index.
Summary: An exploration of the many incredible features and adaptations of the shark, long misunderstood as simply a violent predator. The anatomical details, latest scientific research and wildlife conservation efforts regarding sharks are explored, as well as what made sharks successful predators, how they differ from other animals in their biological success and what unique advantages evolution has conferred on these mythic animals of the deep.
ISBN-13: 978-1-77085-233-4
1. Sharks. I. Title.
597.3 dc23   QL638.9J6754   2013

Library and Archives Canada Cataloguing in Publication
Jorgensen, Salvador
Sharks : ancient predators in a modern sea / Salvador Jorgensen.
Includes bibliographical references and index.
ISBN 978-1-77085-233-4
1. Sharks. I. Title.
QL638.9.J72 2013   597.3   C2013-901245-1

Published in the United States by   Published in Canada by
Firefly Books (U.S.) Inc.   Firefly Books Ltd.
P.O. Box 1338, Ellicott Station   50 Staples Avenue, Unit 1
Buffalo, New York 14205   Richmond Hill, Ontario L4B 0A7

Subject research and editing: Scott Michael
Editing and index: Gillian Watts
Cover and interior design: Hartley Millson
Illustrations (pages 50, 54 and 62): George A. Walker

Printed in Canada

To my loving wife, Cheryl, and newborn son Milo.

Contents

Introduction

I could hear another boat approaching, to the south, near the seamount peak. I heard the metallic trill of the anchor chain running out over the rail as the hook dropped to the seabed. A few minutes later there was the sound of scuba divers plunging into the water, and then their scratchy inhalations and bubbly exhalations — like a team of underwater Darth Vaders. I looked across at my dive partner Luke. Maybe they would flush out the sharks in our direction this time. He seemed to be thinking the same thing. Hammerheads hate bubbles.

We had been crouched down, hunkered on the flank of the seamount, for 53 minutes, one on either side of a small ravine under 25 meters (80 feet) of water. Every so often a group of seven large hammerhead sharks would swim cautiously through the ravine. Their muscular flanks rippled languidly, reflecting a silvery light that highlighted their exquisite form and underlying power.

We had our tagging poles ready, with pop-up satellite tags that would track their migratory habits. We were diving with rebreathers — closed-circuit scuba systems — so we were silently inhaling the same warm air over and over, through a loop that filtered out carbon dioxide and added oxygen. The sharks didn't notice us, and neither did the divers. It was peaceful; we were simply waiting for a shark to swim close enough to attach the transmitter tags. They were just so wary in these small groups.

I wondered what it must have been like here at the Espiritu Santo seamount 20 years earlier, when the scalloped hammerhead schools were so massive you could not count all the sharks. In the three years since starting my PhD research, in 2000, I had made more than a hundred dives at this site. Most days there were only a handful of these beautiful sharks. You had to go way out to sea, to isolated islands — Cocos, the Revillagigedos or the Galápagos Islands — to see those big schools now.

On the way out to the seamount from La Paz we had motored past a beach where fishermen cleaned their meager catches. There were piles of hammerhead shark heads — tiny ones. They were from baby sharks, each no larger than my arm. It was a regular sight: baby shark heads at the tide line. As we waited at the seamount, looking across at each other, then scanning around, I wondered when a big school would come by again.

My infatuation with sharks had begun long before, but that dive was a turning point. Somehow I felt for the first time the true fragility of these creatures. It suddenly sank in that these powerful, majestic and feared apex predators were also vulnerable. Maybe it was the circumstances of the dive: sitting motionless for hours, silently watching the ocean from within. Feeling part of the reef, part of the seamount rock, witnessing ocean life as the seamount had, over a geological timescale. Watching boats come and sharks go. I thought, *I should not be among the last to witness this.* How much more important and beautiful a shark is in the ocean than in an expensive bowl of soup.

Sharks are beasts we love to fear. There is some essence about them that has captivated us all, a spell that was probably cast the first time a human ever encountered a shark — legends were born. Since that first encounter, we have learned so much about sharks. We have learned of their migrations, their dietary preferences and the strange, intimate details of their reproduction. The more we learn, the more we are fascinated. We can't get enough.

But perhaps the most surprising thing we have learned is that sharks are generally in trouble worldwide. How could this be? How could our beloved demons now need our protection? What happened, and why do we care? To appreciate this we need to take a step back and consider sharks in their evolutionary context.

What gives sharks their unique "sharkness"? They differ from other fishes (teleosts, the bony fishes) in several key ways. Sharks are from a much older lineage of cartilaginous fishes known as chondrichthyans, while teleosts populated the oceans, lakes and rivers relatively recently. Interestingly, the number of shark species has remained relatively steady since the explosive arrival of teleosts, and sharks have maintained their position as top predators in nearly every ocean environment, from the deep sea to shallow coastal bays. In other words, there are very few fishes, other than sharks themselves, that regularly eat sharks.

Sharks' illustrious evolution through 400 million years of competition and mass extinction events suggests a successful model — the Permian-Jurassic mass extinction event (about 252 million years ago) wiped out 96 percent of all other marine species. A number of unique features that sharks have retained through it all may account for their success.

Sharks' flexible bodies give them an efficient yet powerful mode for moving and capturing prey in their liquid world. They have retained a flexible cartilaginous core skeletal structure that is little more than a vertebral column, large jaws and fingerlike cartilage rays in their fins. Their powerful swimming stroke is delivered from the muscles to a tough skin shell; their bodies essentially "inflate" as the muscles flex, becoming rigid like a car tire, then quickly becoming fluid again as the muscles relax. This ultimately makes their movements very energetically efficient: sharks can patrol for long periods while exerting a minimal amount of energy, waiting for the opportunity to feed. When the opportunity finally presents itself, their bodies can deliver a burst of speed and a powerful bite — since such opportunities come infrequently, sharks must make the most of them.

Each shark tooth has a roll of "spares" behind it in case one is lost. Regular replacement ensures that they are always sharp and ready. By contrast, mammalian predators have one set of teeth for life. If a lion somehow loses its canine teeth during a fight or a struggle with its prey, it will starve.

Another unique adaptation of sharks is the use of liver oil for the dual purposes of buoyancy and energy storage. Ocean animals that live suspended in the water have to contend with controlling their buoyancy. Most teleost fishes have an air bladder that inflates or deflates, depending on their depth, to maintain neutral buoyancy. This is not unlike a hot-air balloon, which blasts hot air to rise but then has to purge air to keep from rising further once the desired altitude has been reached. Instead of an air bladder, sharks have an enlarged liver filled with oil. Since oil is lighter than water, it counteracts their heavy muscles just enough to make sharks slightly denser than water; if they stopped swimming, they would sink slowly. If teleost swim bladders are like hot-air balloons, sharks are like airplanes: they need to keep swimming to maintain their altitude — their depth in the water. Their large fins, like the wings of an airplane, generate lift and help keep them at the desired depth. And the oil in their livers has another advantage: it serves as an energy storage bank. Sharks can build up energy stores during times of abundance and draw on those reserves during leaner times or when feeding is suspended, for example, during migration.

The refinement of these unique features over millions of years has made for highly efficient predators. There is an apex shark predator in every oceanic ecosystem. In the deep ocean, where there is not enough light to tell night from day and the passage of time has no seasonal rhythm, the frilled, megamouth and goblin sharks patiently reign. In the surface waters of the open ocean, where there is no shelter, oceanic whitetips, blue sharks and makos roam widely. Over the coral reefs of the tropical oceans, blacktip and grey reef sharks carry out their patrols. Under the Arctic ice, Greenland and salmon sharks have found ways to keep from freezing while profiting from the area's rich food sources. We can find a refined, efficient shark predator anywhere in the ocean.

A delicate balance exists between the evolution of ever more refined predatory efficiency and the danger of overwhelming a prey source. Enough prey must be able to escape and reproduce to maintain a large enough population to continually support the predators. In this respect, a less visible adaptation of sharks is their slow growth and reproductive rates and late maturity. These important life-history traits control how fast shark populations are able to grow. Slow population growth may be vital for apex predators that have no real predators themselves — vital for keeping their numbers in check. However, it is no longer true that sharks generally have no predators. Humans now consume up to 100 million sharks annually.

Some of their key predatory adaptations have earned sharks our fear, respect and even hatred. Personification of these traits has shaped societies' perception of sharks in ways that perpetuate their demonization. Their constant slow swimming — necessary to keep them afloat and breathing — is perceived as a cold relentlessness. Their sudden shifting from this restful pace to an elevated state of prey pursuit has been dubbed "shark frenzy." Their enhanced sensory abilities, especially their sense of smell, have been exaggerated into such characteristics as a supernatural ability to detect a single drop of blood across vast expanses of water. Large sharks are referred to as "man-eaters," giving the impression that their serrated teeth were designed specifically for that task. And their large dorsal fin has become a visual cue that instantly alerts us to a stalking, lurking danger, a symbol so strong that we instantly hear the ominous *ba-dum, ba-dum* of a certain musical score at first sight.

These perceptions were perhaps most famously shaped and exploited by Peter Benchley and Steven Spielberg, in the cinematic masterpiece *Jaws*. Since its blockbuster success in 1975, the film's depiction of sharks has become so embedded in the human psyche that it is difficult for people to understand or even care that these animals are now threatened and need to be protected. A call to "save the sharks" does not have quite the same ring as "save the whales" because the very word *shark* conjures up so many negative associations. A common response to this call is "the only good shark is a dead shark," and many would say that the world is safer without them. However, when compared with the 100 million sharks killed annually by humans, the average of 6 humans killed by sharks in a year suggests that they are not as dangerous to humans as we are to them.

The same adaptations that made sharks so successful for so long may now be contributing to their demise. Today they are being hunted heavily to satisfy the shark-fin soup industry. Those same large fins that propelled them successfully through the oceans for hundreds of millions of years are fetching exorbitant prices in today's market. They are eaten in broth for the texture of the cartilage inside, and perhaps for the symbolic sense of power associated with eating such a formidable predator. Until the discovery of a successful formula for synthetic vitamin A, sharks were also killed for the oil in their massive livers, which is rich in the vitamin. Heavy exploitation of fish species is less problematic if their populations can regrow quickly, but sharks' adaptations for slow population growth mean that they generally cannot multiply fast enough to keep up with current fishing pressure. Finally, despite a growing recognition of their threatened plight, it is hard for people to sympathize with sharks and support the cause for their protection, because of their reputation as dangerous and ruthless killers.

Through this book we will trace the evolution of the modern sharks (Selachimorpha) — a superorder under the Elasmobranchii subclass — and tour the different ocean habitats in a survey of the diversity of shark species in existence today. Then we will look more closely at the unique adaptations that distinguish sharks from other fishes and highlight the key life-history strategies that likely contributed to sharks' long reign at the top of the food chain, as one of the most ancient vertebrate lineages. We will examine attributes that are outwardly visible — the shape and functions of their bodies for swimming and pursuing and capturing prey — as well as those that are less visible but equally important, including their modes of reproduction. Both these outer and inner aspects of shark biology affect the way sharks behave; we will consider some of the defining aspects of shark behavior. Finally, we will examine how sharks are threatened today in the context of the recent rise of a new super predator — humans.

The Diversity of Sharks

1

What defines a shark, and why have they been so successful? We know a shark when we see one. Even before we have consciously formed a thought, our brain is reflexively screaming, *Shark!* What is it that makes this animal so distinctive, so compelling? Why does it instantly command our attention, our respect, our primal fears? To find the answers, we must begin by looking back 500 million years.

Our understanding of ancient ocean life has been re-created from fossil evidence. The first mobile predators to graduate from scurrying along the bottom of the primordial sea were nautiloids, ancient relatives of the squid. Then gradually the first vertebrates — fishes — evolved to compete with and perhaps prey upon these early cephalopods. The initial wave of fishes comprised jawless creatures, the agnathans (a single descendent group, lampreys and hagfish, persists today). The agnathans were replaced by a second wave of creatures that sported articulated sheets of armor and powerful beak-like plated jaws: the placoderms. But, just like the agnathans before them, the placoderms declined dramatically and became extinct as a third wave emerged. This third speciation wave of fishes consisted of the Chondrichthyes ("cartilage fish"). And, as they say, the third time was the charm.

This third, highly successful group had staying power. It was differentiated by a skeletal jaw studded with continually replaced powerful enamel teeth and tough skin with toothlike scales called dermal denticles. Unlike the previous waves of fish, the chondrichthyans — which include sharks, rays and chimaeras — surged on through global extinction events, thriving for more than 400 million years while countless competitors rose and fell. In fact, chondrichthyans are the oldest surviving organisms that have a vertebral column and jaw; the only vertebrate that is older is the jawless lamprey.

Not only have they been in it for the long haul, sharks have remained relatively unchanged in their basic form, despite upheavals in the earth's climate, drastic changes in prey species and the arrival of new competitors. Their ancient morphology is a reflection of past evolutionary challenges but is adapted today to their contemporary environment, in which they must compete with and prey upon the more advanced modern bony fish species, the teleosts. Even so, sharks persist as apex predators in virtually all the diverse aquatic environments on Earth.

Today we share the planet with well over 1,000 chondrichthyan species, including some 500 modern sharks, and new species are still being discovered. These species reflect elegant and surprising variations on the successful basic shark body plan; each seems customized to thrive in its unique environment,

from the deep sea to shallow reef tide pools. Sharks have evolved to exploit a huge and diverse range of prey items, from plankton to whales. They have even extended their reign to some of the more challenging and inhospitable reaches of the ocean, where other predators cannot survive. They have accomplished this through gradual evolution and refinement of the basic body plan, which has resulted in some unique and at times astonishing forms. Today an impressively diverse array of shark species prevails throughout the oceans' distinctive niches, successfully targeting the wide variety of prey sources available in the present-day seas.

A lemon shark (*Negaprion brevirostris*) becomes active at dusk. One of the factors that have made sharks so successful is their ability to hunt in the dark. In dim lighting, the diverse suite of senses that sharks possess provides them with a sensory advantage over many other species, allowing them to successfully locate, pursue and capture prey in low light conditions.

Requiem sharks (family Carcharhinidae) are the quintessential shark. They embody the sleek, minimalist, compelling form that first comes to mind when imagining a shark. Perhaps this is because they make up one of the largest and most successful families of sharks, occurring in nearly every marine habitat in tropical to warm temperate seas. Many of the Requiem sharks look similar and are difficult to distinguish. One of these, the Caribbean reef shark (*Carcharhinus perezi*) pictured here, is ubiquitous around coral reefs in tropical Western Atlantic. As an apex predator, they are thought to play a major role in shaping Caribbean reef communities.

Diverse Forms: The Shark Family Tree

Initially, scientists based the tricky task of distinguishing groups of shark species on subtle similarities or differences in tooth and body morphology. Recent advances in molecular genetic analysis have since added another dimension to the measure of relatedness. As a result of genetic sequence comparisons, rays and skates (Batoidea) are no longer considered a branch of the shark "clan" on the family tree; rather, they form a separate lineage. That is, batoids and sharks (Selachii) share a common ancestor, but the successful descendants of some particularly fit early sharks branched off and eventually fanned out as numerous distinct shark species. Present-day sharks, the selachians, comprising some 500 species, are the batoids' nearest relatives but form their own subdivision.

The Selachii subdivision, is neatly split between two superorders: Squalomorphii (from *squalidus*, Latin for "rough" or "unpolished") and Galeomorphii (from the Greek for "shark form"). The Galeomorphs are comprised of four orders, and there are either four or five orders of Squalomorphs depending on whether the taxonomic classification is based on body morphology or genetic sequence respectively.

A resident of one of the ocean's most diverse habitats, the coral reef ecosystem, the tassled wobbegong (*Eucrossorhinus dasypogon*) shark resembles the coral on which it rests. Unwary fishes often cannot distinguish the shark from the reef until it is too late.

Shark Phylogeny

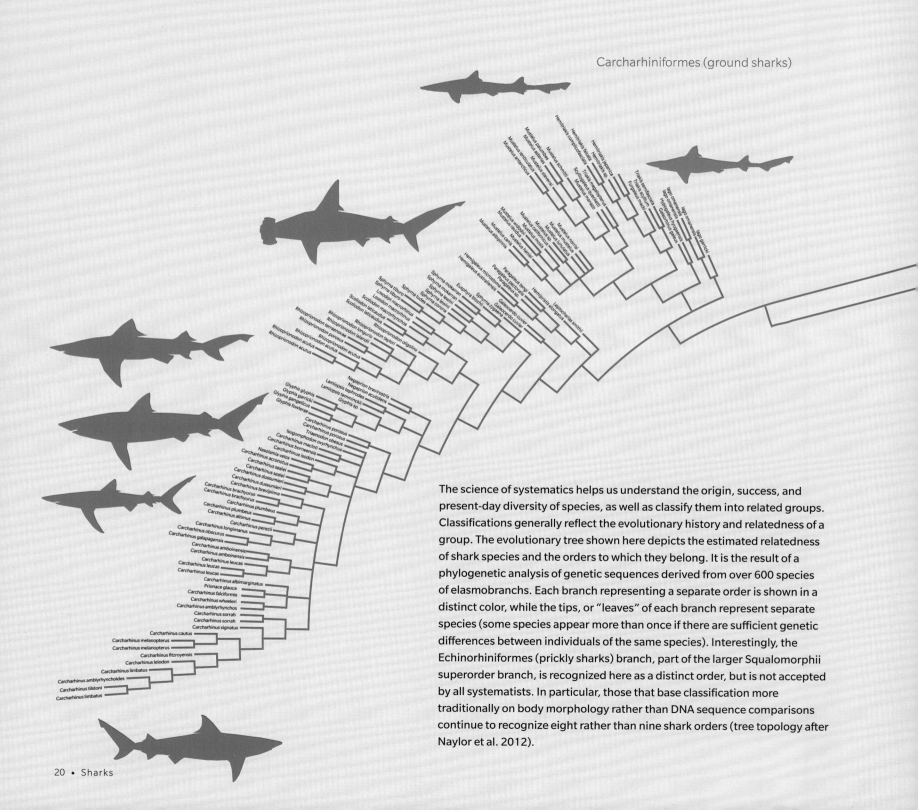

Carcharhiniformes (ground sharks)

The science of systematics helps us understand the origin, success, and present-day diversity of species, as well as classify them into related groups. Classifications generally reflect the evolutionary history and relatedness of a group. The evolutionary tree shown here depicts the estimated relatedness of shark species and the orders to which they belong. It is the result of a phylogenetic analysis of genetic sequences derived from over 600 species of elasmobranchs. Each branch representing a separate order is shown in a distinct color, while the tips, or "leaves" of each branch represent separate species (some species appear more than once if there are sufficient genetic differences between individuals of the same species). Interestingly, the Echinorhiniformes (prickly sharks) branch, part of the larger Squalomorphii superorder branch, is recognized here as a distinct order, but is not accepted by all systematists. In particular, those that base classification more traditionally on body morphology rather than DNA sequence comparisons continue to recognize eight rather than nine shark orders (tree topology after Naylor et al. 2012).

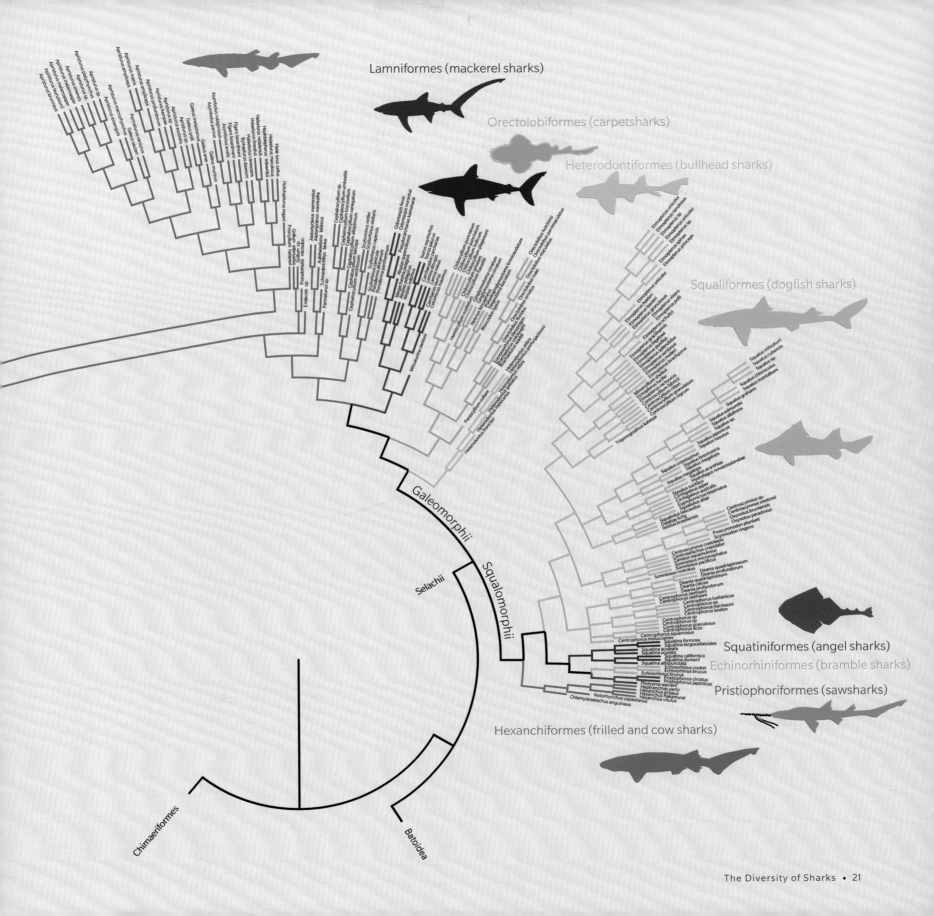

Lamniformes (mackerel sharks)

Orectolobiformes (carpetsharks)

Heterodontiformes (bullhead sharks)

Squaliformes (dogfish sharks)

Galeomorphii

Squalomorphii

Selachii

Squatiniformes (angel sharks)

Echinorhiniformes (bramble sharks)

Pristiophoriformes (sawsharks)

Hexanchiformes (frilled and cow sharks)

Chimaeriformes

Batoidea

Squalomorphii

Hexanchiformes: Cow Sharks and Frilled Sharks
2 families; 4 genera; 6 species

Sharks in the order hexanchiformes are generally considered to be the most primitive group of extant sharks, yet despite their long evolutionary history they are one of the least understood groups of sharks. They are characterized by one or two extra pairs of gill slits, an anal fin and a single dorsal fin located far back on the body. The teeth in the upper jaw are awl-like, while those in the lower are spiked like a cockscomb. The smallest species, the sharpnose sevengill shark (*Heptranchias perlo*), reaches 1.4 meters (4.6 feet), while the largest, the bluntnose sixgill shark (*Hexanchus griseus*) tops out at around 4.8 meters (16 feet).

The hexanchoids live in cool temperate waters or exhibit tropical submergence — they are found at greater depths in warm tropical waters. The bluntnose sixgill is usually found at depths greater than 100 meters (330 feet) and may be found as deep as 2,000 meters (6,600 feet). It does sometimes stray into shallow water; one juvenile specimen was taken 30 kilometers (19 miles) up a river in Tasmania. The broadnose sevengill shark (*Notorynchus cepedianus*) is more often found in coastal habitats.

The adult bluntnose sixgill shark is considered to be a top predator on deep continental shelves and upper slopes around the world, while the broadnose sevengill is an important apex predator along temperate coastlines in the northwestern and southwestern Pacific Ocean, as well as in the South Atlantic. *Hexanchus griseus* regularly feeds on hagfishes, bony fishes and other sharks and may feed on marine mammals in some areas.

The two species of frilled sharks (*Chlamydoselachus*) are placed in their own order by some systematists, and these sharks are certainly very distinct from their hexanchoid relatives the cow sharks. They are more elongate and have terminal mouths and frilly-margined gill slits, the first pair of which extend around the throat and jaws, that narrow toward the tip. The African frilled shark (*Chlamydoselachus africanus*) preys heavily on deepwater catsharks, which it may capture on or near the seafloor; it may also follow them as they make mesopelagic migrations at night and feed on them in mid-water. In Japan the frilled shark (*Chlamydoselachus anguineus*) also eats small fishes and squid. Frilled sharks give birth to small litters, usually 2 to 12 pups, after an incredibly long gestation period — around 3.5 years! While these sharks are typically solitary animals,

OPPOSITE PAGE: The bluntnose sixgill shark (*Hexanchus griseus*) is an important predator in the ocean depths, being the most common large shark on deep slopes (it is usually found below 100 meters [330 feet]) in both tropical and temperate seas. While it spends most of its time moving slowly over the seafloor, it is capable of bursts of speed. Its diet includes some fast-moving bony fishes and other sharks and rays, as well as cetaceans.

34 *C. anguineus* were captured in a single trawl near a mid-Atlantic seamount, suggesting that at least sometimes they congregate to feed or mate. Studies conducted off Japan indicate that this species may segregate by sex, with males occurring in one area and females in another.

A broadnose sevengill shark (*Notorynchus cepedianus*) swims through a kelp forest off South Africa. Sevengill and sixgill sharks, collectively called cow sharks, are generally deepwater species, but the broadnose sevengill shark is found in shallow coastal habitats, where it is an important predator of fish, elasmobranchs and marine mammals. When hunting larger prey such as marine mammals, broadnose sevengills have been observed to hunt cooperatively in packs. Sometimes the tables are turned and the sevengill goes from being hunter to hunted — in several locations they are regularly eaten by killer whales.

1 family; 2 genera; 7 species (at least one species awaiting description)

The Pristiophoriformes are unique sharks that have a bladelike snout, or rostrum, edged with "teeth" (actually modified dermal denticles). At first glance they look like sawfish (rays in the family Pristidae) but are easily distinguished by long barbels located under the snout, as well as the varying sizes of their rostral (snout) teeth, which alternate between long and short. If a sawshark should lose a rostral tooth, a new one will grow back, which is not the case in sawfishes. In the only species in the genus *Pliotrema*, the sixgill sawshark, the rear edges of the large rostral teeth also have serrations. The sawsharks have two dorsal fins; no anal fin; long lateral folds that run along the tail; large spiracles behind the eyes; and five or six pairs of gill slits on the sides of the head (these are under the head in sawfish). The largest species reaches 1.4 meters (4.6 feet) in length.

The sawsharks are found in temperate and tropical seas in the western North Atlantic, Western Pacific and western Indian Oceans. Most occur in deep water on the outer continental shelf or upper slopes. The greatest depth recorded for the order is 915 meters (3,020 feet). The long barbels, together with electro-sensors on the undersurface of the snout, are used to locate their prey, which includes small fishes, crustaceans and squid. While such behavior has not been observed in sawsharks, their batoid counterparts wield their long, tooth-studded rostrum to stun or impale fish.

An eastern sawshark (*Pristiophorus* sp.) foraging over a sandy bottom can use both the electrosensing organs along the length of its rostrum and its sensitive barbels to detect buried prey. Once prey are located, the rostrum may be used to great effect excavating and pining its quarry against the bottom until subdued.

Sawsharks

The "saw" on a sawshark is an elongated rostrum (snout) that bears teeth along its sides. Amazingly, this peculiar extension evolved in elasmobranchs at least three separate times, in sharks and in rays. The serrated protrusion is not actually used for sawing; it may be used to excavate or pin prey to a sandy or muddy bottom, to strike mobile prey mid-water or for general defense. Today this form exists in two lineages: those in the order of sawsharks (Pristiophoriformes), which are true modern sharks, and in the genus *Pristis*, comprising four species in the order of rays, or batoids.

There are six described species of sawshark. The most recently described, *Pristiophorus delicatus*, was discovered only in 2008. Sawsharks are smaller than their distant sawfish ray cousins, which are much more familiar because of their larger size and their distribution in shallow waters, including coastal rivers and lagoons. The teeth of the saw developed from modified dermal denticles (the "scales" of a shark), but the saw also has a sensitive side. It is lined top and bottom with ampullae of Lorenzini, making it an effective electrosensing wand that can detect prey both above and below.

A sawshark (*Pristiophorus* sp.) swims above the bottom off New South Wales, Australia. Giving birth to babies with a rostrum covered with sharp teeth seems like a losing prospect for mother sawsharks. However, these sharks have evolved a clever developmental strategy to circumvent the problem. Although the teeth of young sharks erupt when they are still inside their mother, they lie flat against the rostrum until after birth, at which point they extend into their normal lateral position.

Much like the teeth in other sharks' jaws, rostral teeth in sawsharks are replaced if lost during hunting or in competitive interactions with other sawsharks. Adult sawsharks have been seen with scratches and cuts along their bodies that are thought to be the result of fights with their own kind.

Squalomorphii

Echinorhiniformes: Bramble Sharks
1 family; 1 genus; 2 species

Only two unusual sharks make up the order Echinorhiniformes: the bramble shark (*Echinorhinus brucus*) and the prickly shark (*E. cookei*). Both species are generally slow moving benthic (bottom-dwelling) predators. It is believed that these sluggish sharks catch their prey, primarily fish, smaller sharks and crustaceans, by rapidly expanding their buccal cavity to suck prey into their mouth. Echinorhiniformes have an interesting systematic history. Classification based on genetic analysis only recently placed the bramble sharks in their own order. Previously they belonged as a family within the order Squaliformes. In fact, many experts still do no accept their independent order status. Both bramble shark species are robust and cylindrical in shape, with no dorsal spines or anal fin and two small dorsal fins set far back on the body; the origin of the first dorsal fin is behind that of the pelvic fin, while the opposite is the case in the Squaliformes. Both species have larger denticles than the Squaliformes and other sharks in general; those of the bramble shark (*E. brucus*) are thornlike, with some being fused into groups of two to ten.

The bramble shark produces litters of 15 to 24 and the prickly shark can have up to 114 pups. The prickly shark reaches a length of more than 3 meters (10 feet), while the bramble shark can be more than 4 meters (13.2 feet) long.

The two species are most often found on outer continental shelves or upper slopes, in water as shallow as 15 meters (50 feet) but typically deeper than 100 meters (330 feet); the bramble shark has been captured as deep as 900 meters (2,970 feet). At the head of Monterey Submarine Canyon, off California, divers have a rare opportunity to observe prickly sharks. Groups of these animals aggregate in relatively shallow water, usually from 15 to 40 meters (50 to 132 feet) deep. As many as 40 of these sharks have been seen on a single dive, slowly moving over the seafloor and along the canyon walls or hovering in the water column. Prickly shark in the Monterey canyon show strong site fidelity, resting during the day at specific locations in deep water; at dusk they begin to move up into the water column to feed in mid-water. They begin to return to their diurnal refuge sites at dawn.

The prickly shark (*Echinorhinus cookei*), frequently seen by divers in Monterey Submarine Canyon, is typically indifferent to the presence of air-breathing aquanauts. Both of the *Echinorhinus* species are apex predators that consume sharks, bony fishes, cephalopods and crabs.

Squalomorphii

Squatiniformes: Angel Sharks
1 family; 1 genus; 22 species

At first glance, members of the order Squatiniformes look more like rays than they do sharks. The body is flattened, the pectoral fins are enlarged and the gill slits are not visible from above (they are on the sides of and slightly under the head). But, unlike the rays, these sharks have a "neck" — that is, the pectoral fins are not connected to the head. Also, the mouth is terminal, at the end of the head rather than on its undersurface, as is the case with most rays. Angel sharks have large spiracles, which facilitate respiration. Two dorsal fins are located near the tail; they lack an anal fin. While the upper and lower lobes of the tail are similar in size, the lower lobe is slightly larger. Both the upper and lower jaws are armed with small, needlelike teeth. The largest species reaches around 2 meters (6.6 feet); the males mature sooner and remain smaller than females.

Angel sharks reside on continental shelves and upper slopes down to depths of 1,000 meters (3,300 feet). Because they are substrate-bound and are not strong swimmers, in some species gene flow is reduced between neighboring populations. These sharks are ambush predators that prey most heavily on bony fishes, squid and crustaceans. They lie still on the seafloor, sometimes burying themselves just under the sand or mud to enhance their concealment. They will feed during both day and night but are more active and likely to move to a different hunting ground after dark.

OPPOSITE PAGE: The angel shark (*Squatina squatina*) is a benthic ambush predator that historically was distributed throughout the northeastern Atlantic, ranging from Norway to North Africa and including the Mediterranean. Unfortunately this species has been extirpated from large parts of its historical range because of overfishing. It has the distinction of being one of a handful of sharks listed as critically endangered by the International Union for the Conservation of Nature (IUCN). Like most others in this family, its coloration helps it to disappear when resting or partially buried on the seafloor.

RIGHT: A Japanese angel shark (*Squatina japonica*) buries itself under the sand to avoid detection by predators and prey. A number of angel shark species have been described in the past decade, including this one, and still others are awaiting formal description. While most occur in relatively shallow depths (less than 100 meters/330 feet) on the continental shelf, some species are found on the upper slopes at depths in excess of 1,000 meters (3,300 feet).

Squalomorphii

Squaliformes: Dogfish Sharks
6 families; 22 genera; 129 species

The Squaliformes include both dwarfs and giants. This large order contains the smallest of all known shark species, the dwarf lantern shark (*Etmopterus perryi*), which attains a length of only 16 centimeters (6.3 inches), as well as one of the largest of the non-plankton-eating sharks, the Greenland shark (*Somniosus microcephalus*), which may exceed 5.5 meters (18 feet). All the members of the order share these characteristics: five pairs of gill slits, two dorsal fins and a first dorsal fin that originates in front of the pelvic fin origin. Many but not all of these sharks have stout spines in front of each dorsal fin, and a large number have light-producing organs (see Chapter 3, page 130).

Squaliformes are broadly distributed from arctic to equatorial waters, although most dwell in cool temperate seas or at great depths in more tropical climes. Many can be found swimming near or in repose on the seafloor. Some inhabit relatively shallow water, while others live in the deeper mesopelagic or even the bathypelagic zone. Some deepwater Squaliformes (for example, lantern sharks and cookie-cutter sharks) ascend into the water column at night, typically in response to the vertical migration of their prey. This order also includes some of the deepest-dwelling sharks, such as the Portuguese shark (*Centroscymnus*

The prickly dogfish (*Oxynotus bruniensis*) is an unusual deepwater dogfish that spends its day swimming just above the seafloor. It will occasionally hover over the bottom, using its pectoral fins to help maintain its position in the water column, and place its snout on the substrate. From this position it will suck in sediment and polychaete worms, a favored food, from the mud. Its close relative the rough prickly dogfish (*Oxynotus centrina*) is seen in Turkish waters at safe diving depths as shallow as 35 meters (116 feet).

coelolepis), which is usually found in water at least 400 meters (1,320 feet) deep and has been reported at depths of 3,675 meters (12,128 feet).

The diet of the Squaliformes varies, being in part a function of the species size. The more diminutive dogfishes feed on squid and small bony fishes, while the larger types, such as sleeper sharks (*Somniosus* species), live on a highly eclectic diet ranging from marine snails to heftier and more challenging quarry such as giant squid and marine mammals. How these lethargic sleeper sharks capture alert and fast-moving prey remains a mystery.

The North Pacific spiny dogfish (*Squalus suckleyi*) is a very slow-growing, long-lived species. It matures at around 24 years and may live as long as 100 years. In addition it produces only between 2 and 12 pups in a litter, and its two-year gestation period is one of the longest in the animal world. As a result, this species can sustain only a very low level of fishing pressure and is very susceptible to overfishing.

Galeomorphii

Heterodontiformes: Bullhead Sharks
1 family; 1 genus; 9 species

As the name *bullhead sharks* suggests, the Heterodontiformes have a short, blunt snout, a conical head and eyes that are set high on the head, keeping the sharks out of harm's way when they feed on spiny prey such as sea urchins. The family and genus names (*heterodontus* means "different teeth") refer to the variation in dentition along the jaw. The teeth in the front are small, with cusps, but as you move back along the jaw, the teeth become larger and molar-like. Another common name ascribed to this group is "horn sharks," in reference to the stout spine in front of each dorsal fin. Unlike the dogfish, which may have a single dorsal fin spine, bullheads are the only shark species with a space in front of both dorsal fins. They have five pairs of gill slits and strong grooves that run from the nostrils into the mouth.

The bullheads are small to medium-sized sharks, with the largest species reaching 1.7 meters (5.6 feet). All the species produce unique egg cases that have an auger-like flange; in a few species there are also tendrils on one end of the egg capsule. Survivability of the developing embryos of at least one member of the group, the Port Jackson shark (*Heterodontus portusjacksoni*), is low; as many as 80 percent of the eggs have their contents eaten by boring snails, other bullhead sharks, large stingrays or wrasses.

OPPOSITE PAGE: The Port Jackson shark (*Heterodontus portusjacksoni*), an egg-layer, is found only in Australia. Female sharks have been observed swimming with their eggs in their mouths, searching for a safe location to deposit them. Typically that location is rock crevices, although egg cases have been found in other locations, including inside tin cans lying on the bottom. This may be the only instance of parental care in sharks.

RIGHT: The egg cases of a Port Jackson shark being eaten by a closely related crested Port Jackson shark (*Heterodontus galeatus*). While the leathery egg case may provide some protection from predators, other sharks, stingrays, snails and certain bony fishes still manage to get to the nutritious contents within.

Heterodontiformes are found in the warm temperate and tropical Pacific to western Indian Oceans. They reside on continental and insular shelves and on the uppermost slopes, occurring in tide pools to depths of 275 meters (908 feet). They feed primarily on hard-shelled invertebrates, especially crabs and sea urchins. Their incredibly strong jaws and crushing teeth facilitate mastication of their preferred prey.

Galeomorphii

Orectolobiformes: Carpetsharks
7 families; 13 genera; 43 species

The Orectolobiformes comprise a fascinating group that contains some of the most ornate and beautifully marked of all shark species. Their common name is said to come from their attractive color patterns, which are reminiscent of an Oriental carpet. All of these sharks have five pairs of gill slits, small to large spiracles just below the eyes, an anal fin, two dorsal fins that lack spines, and a tail with a well-developed upper lobe and a poorly developed lower lobe — excluding the whale shark, which has a more typical heterocercal tail. The carpetsharks have a short mouth located in front of the eyes; in many species it is connected to the nostrils by grooves. Some species, notably the wobbegongs, have skin flaps around the head that help break up their outline, and which conceal them from their prey. Some species have distinctive barbels; as nurse sharks grub among rubble and reef interstices, these sensory organs aid them in finding concealed prey. The teeth are relatively small and can consist of a single sharp cusp or multiple stout cusps suited for grasping their prey. While many of the carpetsharks are more diminutive — less than 1 meter (3.3 feet) — the group also includes the largest known fish: the whale shark, which is reported to reach a length of 20 meters (66 feet).

The whale shark is the most fecund of all elasmobranchs, producing as many as 300 pups at a time, but most live-bearing carpetsharks give birth to much smaller litters of 4 to 37 pups. Egg-laying carpetsharks — collared carpetsharks, longtailed carpetsharks and zebra sharks — lay an egg case that is purse-shaped, often with hairlike fibers on the sides that help anchor the egg case to the seafloor.

The Orectolobiformes occur on continental and insular shelves, and many live on coral or rocky reefs. Most members of the order feed on a variety of benthic invertebrates and small fishes. Some, like the wobbegongs, are master ambush predators, while nurse sharks will suck prey from reef crevices by expanding their large pharynx. The whale shark is one of three plankton-feeding sharks (see Chapter 4, page 166, for more on its feeding behavior). Many of the Orectolobiformes are not strong swimmers and spend most of their time on the seafloor. Some wiggle over the bottom in eel-like fashion, while others have modified paired fins that enable them to crawl like a salamander. The whale shark is pelagic and a strong swimmer, capable of crossing ocean basins.

TOP: The spotted wobbegong shark (*Orectolobus maculatus*) is commonly found on rocky reefs off the east coast of Australia. They are generally considered to be sluggish, relatively inactive sharks that rest during the day. There is evidence that they may have favorite nooks, repeatedly returning to specific daytime resting spots. They have also been observed actually wiggling, barely submerged, from one tide pool to another.

BOTTOM: Colclough's shark (*Brachaelurus colcloughi*) is a poorly known member of the carpetshark order that has a very limited geographical range; it is known only from the Queensland and northern New South Wales coasts of Australia. It resides on rocky coastal reefs, often in shallow water less than 30 meters (100 feet) deep, where it feeds mainly on small fishes. The litter size for this diminutive shark is small, usually 6 to 7 pups.

Galeomorphii

Lamniformes: Mackerel Sharks
7 families; 10 genera; 15 species

The Lamniformes order contains the most notorious of all shark species, the great white shark (*Carcharodon carcharias*), as well as one of the most bizarre — the goblin shark (*Mitsukurina owstoni*). Mackerel sharks have an anal fin and two dorsal fins. The sand tigers (*Carcharias* species), crocodile shark (*Pseudocarcharias kamoharai*) and megamouth shark (*Megachasma pelagios*) have a typical heterocercal caudal fin, while the tails of the fast-swimming mackerel sharks are homocercal, with upper and lower lobes that are similar in size. The thresher sharks exhibit the most extreme tail configuration, with the upper lobe actually equaling or exceeding body length; in these species the tail is important in food gathering.

One unique trait found in some members of this group is an elevated body temperature, or endothermy. This is achieved by countercurrent heat exchangers that work between the arterial and venous blood (see Chapter 3, page 138, for more on this adaptation), producing a higher body temperature that enables these sharks to swim faster and longer and expand their range into colder water. Litter sizes are small, usually two in the sand tiger species, two to four in the thresher sharks, and up to fourteen in the white shark.

Diets vary considerably among the various groups in the order. Sand tigers feed on other sharks, bony fishes and squid. The makos are well-known for tackling billfishes, but they more often eat smaller sharks and schooling bony fishes, while the goblin shark is a sluggish deep-sea predator that feeds mainly on bony fishes, supplementing its diet with squid and benthic crustaceans. Adult white sharks have a special taste for marine mammals, while young whites are primarily shark- and fish-eaters. The two most specialized feeders in this order are the basking shark, which is a ramjet plankton feeder, and the megamouth, which uses its jaws like a hoop net to capture swarming crustaceans and sea jellies.

The shortfin mako (*Isurus oxyrinchus*) is one the fastest and most powerful fish in the ocean. Everything about this shark is exquisitely adapted to its open ocean habitat and highly active lifestyle. It preys upon a variety of species, including other large predators such as sharks and billfish. The mako is famous as a game fish; when hooked by fishermen, makos have been observed to jump as high as 6 meters (20 feet) out of the water, a feat that would require a speed of at least 35 kilometers per hour (22 miles per hour).

The cosmopolitan smalltooth sand tiger (*Odontaspis ferox*) is found in all tropical and temperate seas, spending most of its time near the seafloor. While it is normally considered a deepwater species, adults have been found at eight widely separated sites that are within safe diving depths of 15 to 65 meters (50 to 215 feet), including off the coasts of Lebanon, Tanzania, Australia, New Zealand, Colombia and Brazil. Juveniles are thought to spend their time in deeper water than adults, usually on continental slopes deeper than 300 meters (990 feet), where they can avoid competition with and being eaten by other lamnid and large carcharhind sharks.

Bigeye Thresher

The bigeye thresher (*Alopias superciliosus*) is one of the most notable shark species. Not only does it possess a scimitar-shaped tail as long as its body, it also has the largest eye, relative to body size, of any vertebrate except birds. Its large diameter maximizes the eye's light-capturing capabilities, and it is also equipped with an "eye heater" that may enhance the shark's vision, giving it a predatory edge in the cold, dark depths. The eye heater is a heat-exchange structure known as an orbital rete, a network of blood vessels that transfers heat from the blood leaving the eye to the new blood just arriving.

Thresher sharks are deep foragers, regularly pursuing their prey down to 500 meters (1,650 feet). At this depth the cold temperatures and low light levels make hunting a challenge, and their special adaptations give thresher sharks an advantage. The only other sharks to have an eye heater are members of the family Lamnidae (salmon, mako and white sharks). Interestingly, the lamnids are thought to have evolved their eye-heating capacity independently from the threshers.

Bigeye threshers occur around the world in tropical and temperate seas, in habitats ranging from coastal to oceanic. Like many pelagic organisms, they exhibit diel (daily) vertical migration: they reside in cold deeper waters — as deep as 300 to 500 meters (990 to 1,650 feet) — during the day and move to warmer, shallower waters near the surface during the night, likely to feed.

The large, upward-looking eyes of bigeye thresher sharks are perfectly suited for their oceanic lifestyle. Their eyes, which are adapted to function at cold temperatures and low light levels, are also able to roll upward, allowing the shark to hunt prey from below by searching for silhouettes illuminated by light filtering down from the surface.

Galeomorphii

Carcharhiniformes: Ground Sharks
8 families; 49 genera; 224 species

The ground shark order is the most species-rich and also the most recently evolved, with most species appearing fewer than 100 million years ago, including a handful of relatively recent species — less than 25 million years old. The order contains the large requiem or whaler shark family (Carcharhinidae), which includes such "classic" sharks as the bull shark (*Carcharhinus leucas*), blue shark (*Prionace glauca*), lemon shark (*Negaprion brevirostris*) and tiger shark (*Galeocerdo cuvier*). But some eccentrics such as the ghost catshark (*Apristurus* species) are also part of this order. Overall the ground sharks include some of the most abundant species. The oceanic whitetip, now greatly reduced, was at one time thought to be one of the most abundant large apex predators on Earth. Ground sharks are also the order most implicated in attacks on humans, although distinguishing which species is responsible has been problematic, since so many Carcharhiniformes look alike, making identification to species difficult.

The unique hammerhead sharks (family Sphyrnidae) also belong to the ground shark order. The nine species of hammerheads are among the most recently evolved of all shark species. Aside from the hammerheads, there is not a huge diversity of form in the ground sharks; most species in this order are very "typical" looking. All ground sharks have two dorsal fins — with one exception, the onefin catshark (*Pentanchus profundicolus*) — an anal fin and five gill slits, the last three located over the pectoral fin base. They also are characterized with eyes that have a nictitating fold or membrane — a movable lower eyelid that can be closed — to help protect the eye when the shark subdues its prey.

The ground sharks are found in shallow coastal habitats (some even enter fresh water), in the open ocean and on continental slopes. The six species in the genus *Glyphis*, known as the river sharks, are most abundant in estuarine and freshwater habitats. And the bull shark is well-known for its habit of traversing rivers, and is found in most major rivers that empty into tropical and subtropical oceans. Many of the smoothhounds (family Triakidae) are found in coastal waters or over the continental shelf. One anomaly in this family is the genus *Iago*, the houndsharks, which prowl on continental slopes at depths of 100 to more than 2,000 meters (330 to 6,600 feet). Most of the catsharks (family Scyliorhinidae) make their home in the ocean depths.

For example, the sawtail catsharks (genus *Galeus*) live on the continental slope, usually deeper than 200 meters (660 feet), while the ghost catsharks

OPPOSITE PAGE: Like many Carcharhiniformes, particularly those of the requiem family, the sandbar shark (*Carcharhinus plumbeus*) is a cosmopolitan coastal species that is found throughout warm temperate and subtropical waters of the Atlantic, Pacific and Indian Oceans in a mosaic of smaller, closely related populations across the globe. Genetic evidence suggests that gene flow between these populations is "mediated" by males — a common scenario for sharks. It is often assumed that male sharks wander and females stay at home. However, the pattern is typically driven by the homing behavior of females, who return to their birthplace to pup (natal philopatry). In many cases it is the females that initially wander and mate with males of adjacent populations, then bring those foreign male genes back when they return to give birth.

occur at depths of more than 500 meters (1,650 feet), with some found as deep as 1,600 meters (5,280 feet).

When it comes to feeding, many of the Carcharhiniformes are opportunistic and eclectic in their tastes. For example, the bull and tiger sharks exhibit wide dietary breadth. However, there are some in the order that are more finicky. For example, the sicklefin weasel shark (*Hemigaleus microstoma*) is primarily a cephalopod-eater, while the bonnethead shark (*Sphyrna tiburo*) is a specialized crab-eater. Young golden hammerheads (*Sphyrna tudes*) feed heavily on crustaceans, while adults eat crustaceans, sea catfishes and their eggs — the carotenoids (orange and reddish pigments) in their prey contribute to the unusual golden coloration of this species.

Current molecular research suggests that the taxonomy of the Carcharhiniformes order is a mess and may be formally rearranged soon. When all is said and done, the order may end up with 14 families and 60 genera, or possibly more. There are also likely more species to be discovered, especially in the more poorly known groups such as the ghost catshark genus *Apristurus* (currently more than 40 species are recognized in this genus).

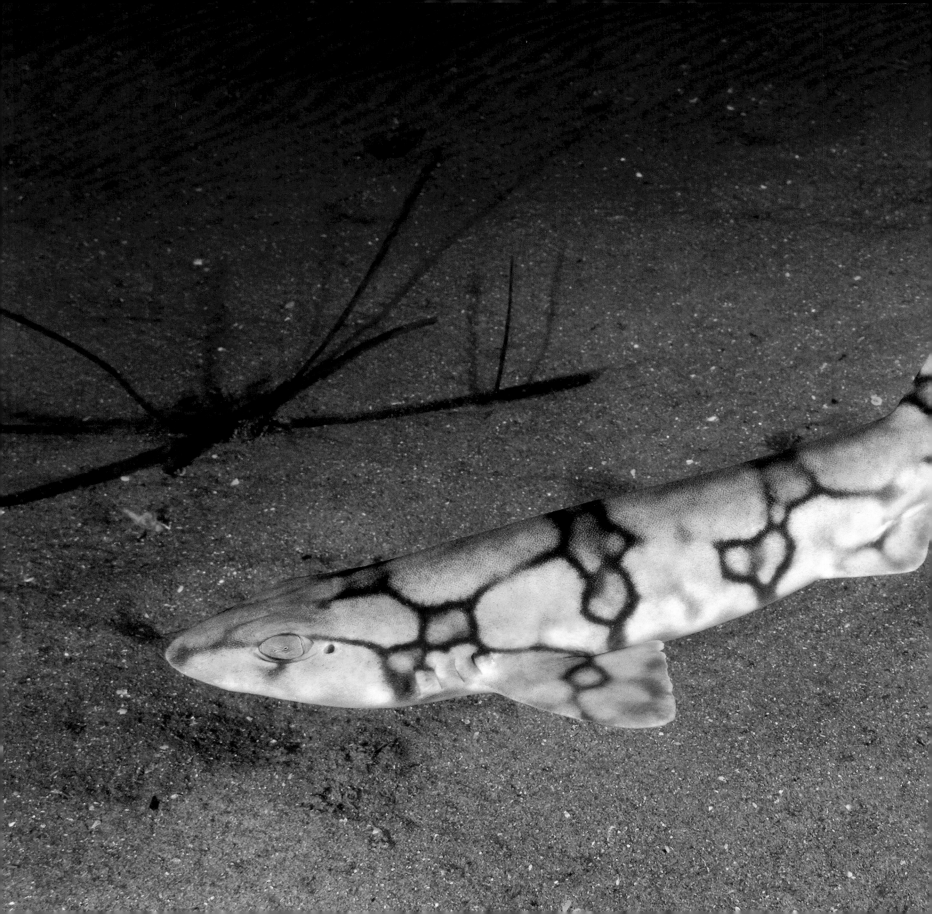

With over 150 species, the catshark family Scyliorhinidae is the most species-rich in the order Carcharhiniformes. Many are beautifully marked, including the chain catshark (*Scyliorhinus retifer*). This species is a resident of deep water on outer continental shelves and slopes in the western North Atlantic. Females lay a pair of egg cases about every 15 days. When the tendrils at the ends of the egg case protrude from the female's cloaca, she drags them around corals or other bottom structures until the egg cases are yanked out. More than one female may use the same oviposition site, so numerous eggs in different stages of development may hang from the same coral. After hatching, the young chain catsharks rest in groups on smooth mud bottoms.

Hammerheads

The hammerhead is the most recognizable of all shark species. Its unique lateral head expansion, called a cephalofoil, has evolved only in this single group, the family Sphyrnidae. The length of the cephalofoil varies by species, from that of the bonnethead (*Sphyrna tiburo*), which extends to 18 percent of its body length, to the winghead shark (*Eusphyra blochii*) at 50 percent. The relatively recent and rapid branching of this family into eight species with distinctive cephalofoil shapes suggests that it is a successful design, but scientists are still uncertain why. One hypothesis is that it provides lift, like an airplane wing, an important function for sharks of this and many other families that need to swim continuously in order to breathe. The underside of the cephalofoil also provides an enlarged area for the electroreceptor organs called the ampullae of Lorenzini, which may enhance their ability to detect the minute electrical fields generated by their prey.

Hammerhead Shark Cephalofoil Comparison

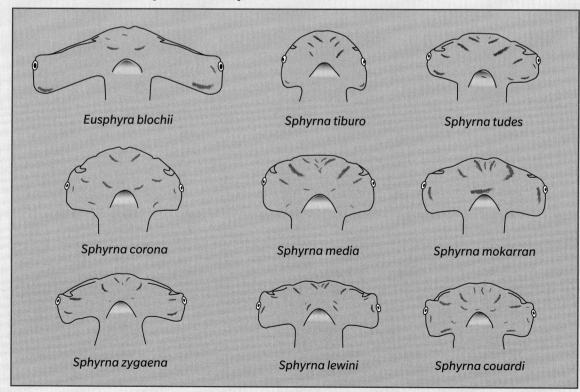

Eusphyra blochii   *Sphyrna tiburo*   *Sphyrna tudes*

Sphyrna corona   *Sphyrna media*   *Sphyrna mokarran*

Sphyrna zygaena   *Sphyrna lewini*   *Sphyrna couardi*

What's in a cephalofoil? A radiographic image of the rostrum of a bonnethead shark (*Sphyrna tiburo*) reveals the cartilaginous skeletal layout and sensory systems (optical, olfactory and electrosensing). These structures do not differ from those of non-hammerhead species in their general layout but have an increased distance between bilateral features (for example, eyes and nostrils) and an increased electroreceptive search area, with a larger total number of electrosensory pores (ampullae of Lorenzini) on the undersides of their cephalofoil.

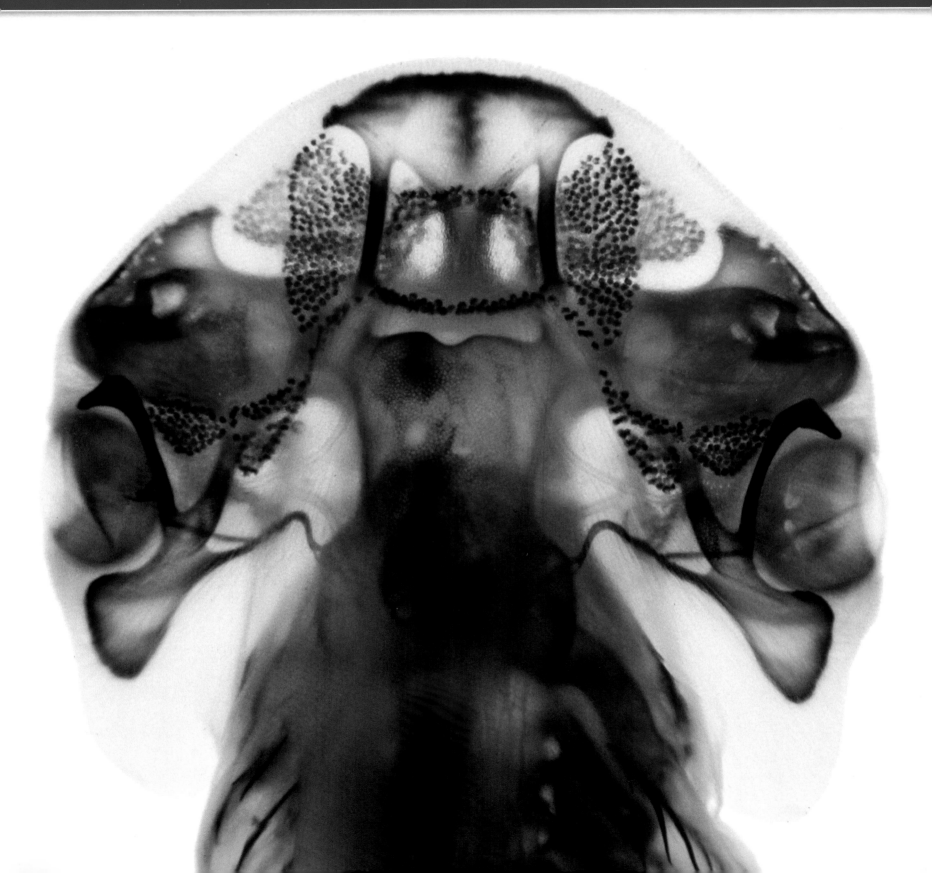

Diverse Habitats

Ocean Zones

The oceans cover some 70 percent of the Earth's surface. And considering that ocean life occurs throughout its volume, not just at the surface, it is a vast and diverse realm supporting numerous shark predators in virtually every ocean ecosystem. A variety of shark species can be found across a wide range of depths, from the ocean's surface down to at least 3,600 meters (12,000 feet), and at different distances from the shore, from the most isolated open ocean areas right up into the shallowest tide pools. Ocean zones are typically distinguished and defined by their distance from land, and by their distance from the surface, or depth.

Regarding distance from shore, the first area at the ocean–land interface that is cyclically exposed and flooded by the tides is the intertidal or littoral zone. A small number of shark species such as the epaulette shark are able to reside there, while others visit only when the tide is high and must retreat when the tides are turned. Beyond the intertidal zone, extending out to the edges of the continental shelf, is the neritic zone. The neritic zone is replete with varying habitats that include estuaries, seagrass beds, bays, coral reefs, rocky reefs, kelp beds and more. This is a diverse and productive portion of the marine environment and home to numerous shark species, including many species that only reside in the protected shallow water as newborns. The vast expanse of open ocean beyond the neritic waters is the pelagic zone. This is the largest ocean zone, a vast open environment with little or no shelter but is home to many actively swimming sharks species.

The ocean can be further categorized by depth, particularly the pelagic zone. The ocean changes drastically with depth due primarily to the rapid extinction of light with increasing distance from the surface. The epipelagic zone — also known as the sunlight or euphotic zone — is the portion of the oceanic water column that extends from the surface to about 200 meters (660 feet). Enough light penetrates this portion of the water column to allow photosynthesis to occur, and as a result there are abundant phytoplankton populations. It is also home to a moderately large shark community. Below the epipelagic zone is the mesopelagic zone, from about 200 to 1,000 meters (660 to 3,300 feet). Light barely penetrates this part of the water column, and it is sometimes referred to as the "twilight zone." Here we find an increase in the abundance of bioluminescent animals, including some glowing sharks. Some sharks live at these depths (or deeper) for most of their lives, including a number of Squaliformes sharks, while others make forays into this zone to exploit feeding opportunities. Below the mesopelagic is the bathypelagic zone — around 1,000 to 3,000 meters (3,300 to 9,900 feet) deep — the most expansive oceanic zone. The sharks that occur here are primarily Squaliformes species, as well as some catsharks, especially the ghost catsharks (*Apristurus* species). The bathypelagic zone is a dark, cold place that is subject to incredible pressure.

The next deepest portions of the water column are the abyssopelagic zone, below 3,000 meters (9,900 feet), and the hadalpelagic zone, from 6,000 meters (20,000 feet) to the deepest ocean canyons. This is an extreme environment populated by fish and invertebrates that have special adaptations. There are few nutrients here, the water is cold (except near hot-water hydrothermal vents), it is dark and the pressure is even more extreme. Neither of these zones is known to be home to many sharks, but a few species do stray into the abyssopelagic zone, including the bluntnose sixgill, Greenland, Portuguese, cookie-cutter and lantern sharks. A handful of other cartilaginous fishes (skates and chimaeras) occur in the upper regions of the abyssopelagic zone.

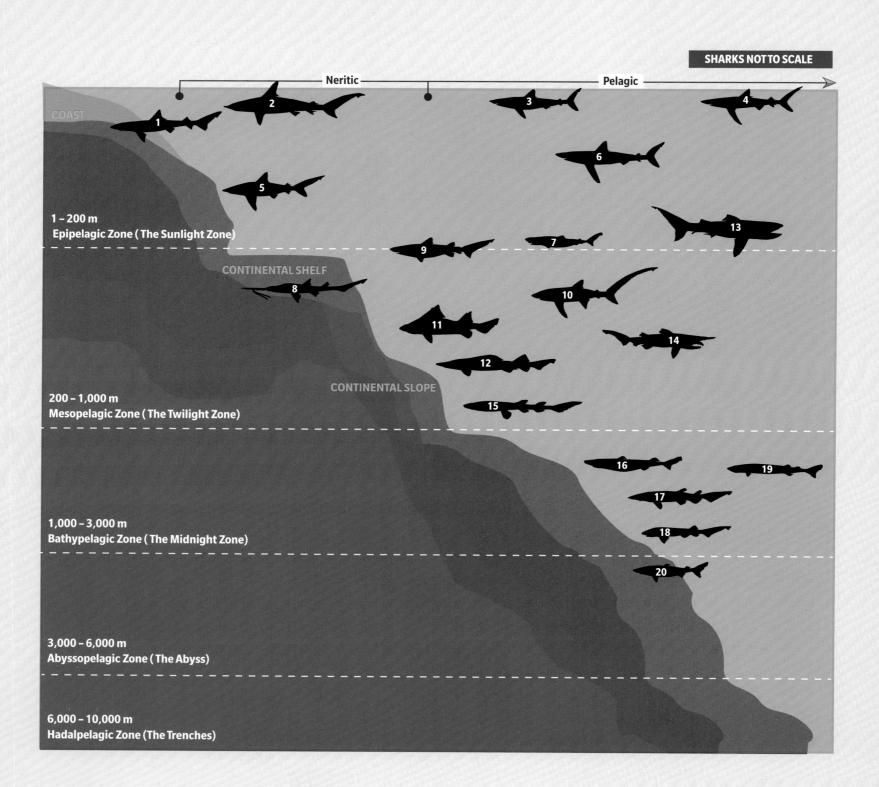

SHARKS NOT TO SCALE

Neritic — Pelagic —→

COAST

1 – 200 m
Epipelagic Zone (The Sunlight Zone)

CONTINENTAL SHELF

200 – 1,000 m
Mesopelagic Zone (The Twilight Zone)

CONTINENTAL SLOPE

1,000 – 3,000 m
Bathypelagic Zone (The Midnight Zone)

3,000 – 6,000 m
Abyssopelagic Zone (The Abyss)

6,000 – 10,000 m
Hadalpelagic Zone (The Trenches)

1. Smoothhound shark (*Mustelus canis*)
Western Atlantic Ocean. Continental shelves and upper slopes from 0 to 579 meters (0 to 1,911 feet); usually at less than 18 meters (59 feet) in US waters and deeper in the Caribbean. Migratory, moving to warmer climes in winter. Litter size 4 to 20.

2. Smooth hammerhead shark (*Sphyrna zygaena*)
Circumglobal in tropical and warm temperate seas. Oceanic, on continental and insular shelves from 0 to 100 meters (0 to 330 feet). Sometimes forms huge migratory schools, moving to warmer waters in winter. Litter size 20 to 49.

3. Shortfin mako shark (*Isurus oxyrhynchus*)
Circumglobal in tropical and warm temperate seas, from 0 to 400 meters (0 to 1,320 feet). Adults will yoyo swim, sometimes diving below thermocline for short periods. Solitary. Litter size 4 to 16.

4. Blue shark (*Prionace glauca*)
Circumglobal in tropical and temperate seas. Oceanic, sometimes inshore near islands, from 0 to 450 meters (0 to 1,485 feet). Makes yoyo dives when seeking prey. Solitary or in aggregations. Litter size 4 to 134.

5. Bignose shark (*Carcharhinus altimus*)
Circumtropical. Edges of continental and insular shelves and upper slopes from 0 to 430 meters (0 to 1,419 feet). Vertical migrator, in deeper water during day and moving into shallow water or near surface in pelagic zone at night. Litter size 3 to 11.

6. Longfin mako shark (*Isurus paucus*)
Circumtropical. Oceanic, from 0 to 200 meters (0 to 660 feet). Little known about its biology. Lifestyle probably more similar to that of blue shark or oceanic whitetip than its faster cousin, the shortfin mako.

7. Crocodile shark (*Pseudocarcharias kamoharai*)
Circumtropical. Oceanic, epipelagic and mesopelagic, from 0 to 300 meters (0 to 990 feet). Possible vertical migrator: large eyes indicate nighttime and deep ocean feeding. Extremely oily liver means near-neutral buoyancy. Litter size 4.

8. Sixgill sawshark (*Pliotrema warreni*)
Temperate and tropical Indian Ocean. Benthic and epibenthic, on continental shelf and upper slopes from 60 to 430 meters (198 to 1,419 feet). Young live at shallower depths than adults. Litter size 5 to 17.

9. Bigeye sand tiger shark (*Odontaspis noronhai*)
Sporadic records in tropical seas in central and southwestern Atlantic and central Pacific Oceans; possibly circumglobal. Epipelagic and mesopelagic, on upper to mid slopes from 60 to 1,000 meters (198 to 3,300 feet). Possibly vertical migrator. Oviphagous. Litter size uncertain, possibly 2.

10. Bigeye thresher shark (*Alopias superciliosus*)
Circumglobal in tropical and warm temperate waters. Epipelagic and mesopelagic. During day occurs at 200 to 500 meters (660 to 1,650 feet) with dives to more than 700 meters (2,310 feet); moves into lesser depths at night, about 10 to 130 meters (33 to 420 feet). Litter size 2 to 4.

11. Angular rough shark (*Oxynotus centrina*)
Eastern Atlantic, British Isles and Mediterranean. Continental shelves and slopes from 50 to 660 meters (165 to 2,178 feet), mostly below 100 meters (330 feet). Moves slowly over bottom, occasionally hovering above seafloor. Litter size 10 to 15.

12. False catshark (*Pseudotriakis microdon*)
Wide-ranging, with sporadic distribution in Atlantic, Indo-Pacific and Western and central Pacific Oceans. Rarely on continental shelves, more often on upper to deep slopes from 200 to 1,900 meters (660 to 6,270 feet). Litter size 2; gestation may be as long as 2 or 3 years.

13. Megamouth shark (*Megachasma pelagicos*)
Circumtropical. Neritic and epipelagic, from 5 to 600 meters (17 to 1,980 feet) but usually 120 to 166 meters (396 to 548 feet). Vertical migrator, moving into shallower depths at night. Solitary.

14. Goblin shark (*Mitsukurina owstoni*)
Sporadic distribution in Western and Eastern Atlantic, western Indian and Western Pacific Oceans. Mesopelagic, on outer continental shelves and upper slopes from 30 to 979 meters (99 to 3,231 feet). Sluggish. May segregate by sex.

15. Lollipop catshark (*Cephalurus cephalus*)
Eastern Pacific. Bathypelagic, on outer shelves and upper to mid slopes from 155 to 927 meters (512 to 3,059 feet). Occurs in hypoxic conditions; enlarged gill cavity is adaptation to living in low-oxygen environments. Litter size 2.

16. Giant lantern shark (*Etmopterus baxteri*)
Southeastern Atlantic, Indo-Pacific and Western Pacific Oceans. Bathypelagic, on upper to mid slopes from 250 to 1,500 meters (820 to 4,920 feet). Segregates by size and sex. Litter size 1 to 16.

17. Deepwater catshark (*Apristurus profundorum*)
Northwestern Atlantic. Bathypelagic, on deep slopes from 1,300 to 1,600 meters (4,290 to 5,280 feet). One of many deepwater members of this genus, known as ghost catsharks. Lays 2 eggs at a time.

18. Bluntnose sixgill shark (*Hexanchus griseus*)
Distribution sporadic in temperate and tropical waters of Atlantic and Indo-Pacific Oceans. Shelves, upper to deep slopes, submarine ridges and seamounts from 0 to 1,875 meters (0 to 6,188 feet); most often found between 500 and 1,100 meters (1,650 to 3,630 feet). Litter size 22 to 108.

19. Cookie-cutter shark (*Isistius brasiliensis*)
Circumglobal in tropical and warm temperate waters. Epipelagic, mesopelagic and bathypelagic, from 0 to 3,500 meters (0 to 11,550 feet). Vertical migrator, moving more than 2,000 meters (6,600 feet) up and down in the water column at night.

20. Portuguese shark (*Centroscymnus coelolepis*)
Wide-ranging in Atlantic and Indo-Pacific Oceans. Outer shelves, upper to deep slopes and abyssal plains from 128 to 3,675 meters (422 to 12,128 feet), but mostly deeper than 400 meters (1,320 feet). Subadults found at greater depths than adults. Adults segregate by sex. Litter size 7 to 16.

The Deep Sea

Over half of all shark species live below 200 meters (660 feet), in the darkness of the deep ocean. They inhabit a slow, frigid, unchanging world. Feeding strategies include scavenging on sinking carcasses, ambush hunting in the dark and migrating toward the surface to feed at night. Sizes vary from the smallest lantern sharks to the giant filter-feeding megamouth shark. The large number of deep-sea species may stem from their isolation. Generally absent below 3,000 meters (about 2 miles), deepwater sharks are absent from the abyssal plains that make up the vast stretches of seafloor between landmasses. Most deep-sea sharks are poor swimmers, and those expanses of deep water present a formidable barrier against migration, so they are confined to the sloping edges of the continents and along the crests of remote oceanic ridges and seamounts. Living in such isolated patches, they have differentiated into numerous distinct species.

Deep-sea sharks are particularly slow-growing, are late to mature and reproduce infrequently. The lack of light and discernible seasonal change in the deep ocean means that many deep-sea sharks do not have specific breeding seasons, making it difficult for scientists to determine gestation periods. Most deep-sea shark mothers carry their young for more than a year, and several species exceed a two-year gestation period.

Discovered in 1976, when an individual became fouled in a navy vessel's sea anchor off Hawaii, the megamouth shark (*Megachasma pelagios*) is a relatively recent discovery and still poorly understood. Since that first one was collected, more than 50 individuals have washed up on beaches or been entangled in fishing gear. It is a circumglobal species, though most specimens have been collected off Japan. The genus name, *Megachasma,* is derived from the Greek *megas* ("large") and *chasma* ("open mouth"), but despite that formidable orifice, this species, along with the basking shark and the whale shark, is a filter feeder that eats krill and other zooplankton. It engages in "suction gulp-feeding," throwing its highly protrusible jaws around swarms of krill, then closing its mouth and expelling the water through its gill slits, straining out the small crustaceans.

The megamouth is a rather flabby beast, with weak body musculature. It is a slow swimmer; the fins are not rigid like those of the basking shark, and its gill openings are not as large. All these characteristics would seem to preclude its feeding like its cousin.

There has been some interesting speculation about the mouth lining of this shark. It appears shiny and luminescent and is thought to possibly act as a light trap, luring swarming zooplankton right up to or even into its enormous jaws. This shark engages in dramatic vertical migrations, moving higher in the water column as the sun sinks and back to greater depths as the dawn light breaks. This is probably a response to the movements of its planktonic prey.

The lantern sharks (family Etmopteridae) are a family of deepwater sharks that include some of the smallest species of living sharks. Most sharks in this family are less than 1 meter (3.3 feet) long, and some are as small as 20 centimeters (8 inches) as adults. This is a large family, with more than 37 species in five genera. A number of the *Etmopterus* species exhibit very limited geographical ranges, while others are more widely distributed. The great lantern shark (*E. princeps*) holds the record for the deepest shark encountered — one was recorded at 4,500 meters (14,850 feet). The maximum age for at least one of the lantern sharks, the New Zealand lantern shark (*E. baxteri*), is estimated to be around 57 years for females. Shown here is a velvet belly lantern shark (*Etmopterus spinax*), photographed in a Norwegian fjord.

The frilled shark (*Chlamydoselachus anguineus*) is the most primitive living shark. Relatively little is known about this living fossil, though it is believed to inhabit very deep water — as deep as 2,500 meters (8,250 feet) — and to migrate to shallower depths during the night, likely to feed. This primitive, eel-like shark reaches a length of 2 meters (6.6 feet) and is named for the frilly appearance of its gill slits, which ring the head like a collar. Its mouth is full of needlelike teeth, ideal for capturing squid, which make up the bulk of its diet in Pacific water off Japan.

Reefs

Nowhere is the diversity of shark species more evident than in tropical reef habitats. Fully one-third of the 465 species of tropical sharks and rays are found in a small geographic area in the Indo-Western Pacific Ocean, consisting of Indonesia, the Philippines, the Malay Peninsula and New Guinea. There are more shark species per unit area in this small region than anywhere else on Earth. This relatively continuous shallow coral reef ecosystem is also home to the highest diversity of tropical reef fishes.

Many carcharhinid sharks, such as the whitetip reef shark (*Triaenodon obesus*), blacktip reef shark (*Carcharhinus melanopterus*), grey reef shark (*C. amblyrhynchos*) and great hammerhead shark (*Sphyrna mokarran*), commonly patrol near or over coral reefs. Meanwhile, numerous benthic sharks blend into the reef structure with their elaborate colors and patterns, including catsharks, wobbegongs, horn sharks, zebra sharks, nurse sharks and longtailed carpetsharks. Seasonal events, such as coral spawning, bring in giant visitors such as the whale shark.

The relative isolation of tropical coral reefs causes separation of populations, which over time become distinct species. As a consequence, many tropical reef shark species are endemic to very specific geographic areas. The best example of this is the genus *Hemiscyllium*, known commonly as epaulette sharks. There are eight members of this genus, and all exhibit very limited ranges in the Indo-Australian region. Colclough's, or the bluegray, carpetshark (*Brachaelurus colcloughi*) is a rocky reef-dweller with a very restricted range — it is endemic to a stretch along Australia's east coast, where its core distribution spans less than 250 kilometers (155 miles).

The small mouth and the structure of the buccal cavity of the nurse shark (*Ginglymostoma cirratum*) allows it to generate tremendous suction, which it uses to great effect when hunting for prey hidden in reef crevices. Nurse sharks have been observed flipping over large conchs and removing the snails from their shells, presumably using this powerful suction. They will also use their bulk to overturn large pieces of rubble and coral colonies as they grub for hidden prey beneath. Juvenile nurse sharks have been observed engaging in an interesting behavior that may serve to attract shelter-seeking prey into strike range: they sit up on their pectoral fins and remain motionless. The space created under the body may lure shrimp or reef fish looking for a place to hide. When they get close enough, the devious nurse shark pounces!

Coral Reef Habitat Preferences

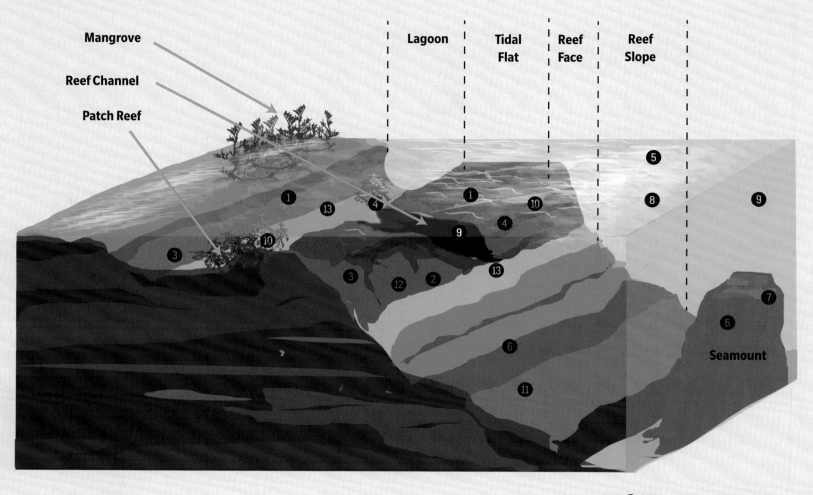

Mangrove

Reef Channel

Patch Reef

Lagoon

Tidal Flat

Reef Face

Reef Slope

Seamount

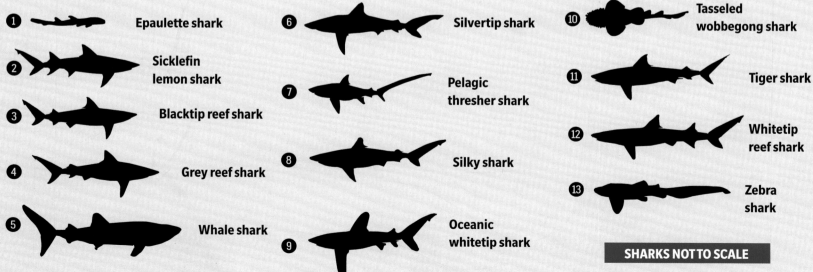

1   Epaulette shark

2   Sicklefin lemon shark

3   Blacktip reef shark

4   Grey reef shark

5   Whale shark

6   Silvertip shark

7   Pelagic thresher shark

8   Silky shark

9   Oceanic whitetip shark

10   Tasseled wobbegong shark

11   Tiger shark

12   Whitetip reef shark

13   Zebra shark

SHARKS NOT TO SCALE

Coral reefs offer a diverse array of habitat types, or zones, and various sharks have evolved as successful predators in each of them. While many shark species occur in a variety of reef zones, others specialize in one or a few specific habitats. Their preferences relate to their unique abilities to exploit particular food sources, limiting competition, and in some cases, to avoiding predators. The conditions in the various zones and their associated microhabitats are highly variable. For example, the reef flat tends to be exposed to more changeable conditions than the reef face. Larger sharks often exploit the reef flat during flood tide, able to forage as the tide rises over areas that were dry just hours before. Then, as the tide recedes they move back into the lagoon or onto the reef face. A few species, such as the epaulette shark, will seek shelter in the pools that remain after the tide goes out. Some sharks use the shallow lagoon or mangroves as a nursery area, to avoid their predatory relatives (including parents). Other species, such as the tiger shark, spend days on deep reef slopes but move into the shallows at night.

1. Epaulette shark (*Hemiscyllium ocellatum*)
Tropical Australia (Great Barrier Reef). Lagoons, back reefs, reef flats and reef faces, 0 to 15 meters (0 to 50 feet) deep. Solitary. Deposit 2 or 3 eggs at a time.

2. Sicklefin lemon shark (*Negaprion acutidens*)
Central Pacific, Western Pacific and Indian Oceans. Lagoons, estuaries, reef flats, reef faces and slopes, 0 to 30 meters (0 to 98 feet) deep. Often found in still, turbid conditions. Juveniles invade tidal flats at flood tide to feed and seek refuge. Litter size 1 to 13.

3. Blacktip reef shark (*Carcharhinus melanopterus*)
Red Sea, east to Society Islands, north to Japan and south to Australia. Lagoons, reef flats, channels, reef faces and slopes, 0 to 20 meters (0 to 65 feet) deep. Solitary. Will aggregate in reef channels at low tide, moving onto reef flat at flood tide. Litter size 3 to 4.

4. Grey reef shark (*Carcharhinus amblyrhynchos*)
East Africa, east to Hawaiian Islands, north to southern Japan and south to Lord Howe Island. All reef habitats, 0 to 274 meters (0 to 891 feet) deep. Solitary or diurnal, in loose groups or polarized schools (group members disperse to hunt after dark). Litter size 1 to 6.

5. Whale shark (*Rhincodon typus*)
Circumglobal in tropical and warm temperate seas. Deep lagoons, reef faces, slopes, seamounts and open ocean, 0 to 1,000 meters (0 to 3,300 feet) deep, but usually 100 meters (330 feet) or less. Makes vertical dives into deep water in open ocean. Migratory. Solitary but aggregates when feeding. Litter size up to 300.

6. Silvertip shark (*Carcharhinus albimarginatus*)
East Africa to Panama, north to Japan and south to Australia. Reef faces, slopes, offshore banks and seamounts, 0 to 40 meters (0 to 130 feet) deep. Occurs singly or in loose groups. Litter size 1 to 11.

7. Pelagic thresher shark (*Alopias pelagicus*)
Warm temperate and tropical Indo-Pacific Ocean. Reef slopes and seamounts but most often open ocean, 1 to 150 meters (3.3 to 488 feet) deep. Solitary. Visits reefs when seeking the cleaning services of wrasses. Litter size 2.

8. Silky shark (*Carcharhinus falciformis*)
Circumtropical. Oceanic but sometimes seen off steep reef faces or slopes, 0 to 500 meters (0 to 1,650 feet) deep. Young often seen in shallower depths than adults. Solitary or in loose groups. Litter size 2 to 14.

9. Oceanic whitetip shark (*Carcharhinus longimanus*)
Circumglobal in tropical and warm temperate seas. Open ocean, but sometimes seen off steep reef faces and slopes, 0 to 150 meters (0 to 495 feet) deep. Usually solitary but will aggregate around food sources. Litter size 1 to 15.

10. Tasseled wobbegong shark (*Eucrossorhinus dasypogon*)
Indonesia, West Papua, Papua New Guinea and northern Australia. Lagoon patch reefs, back reefs, channels, reef faces and slopes, 1 to 40 meters (3.3 to 132 feet) deep. Rests on substrate in open, among corals or in caves and crevices. Solitary.

11. Tiger shark (*Galeocerdo cuvier*)
Circumglobal. Deep lagoons, reef channels, reef faces and slopes, 0 to 305 meters (0 to 991 feet) deep. Adults stay in deeper water during day and move into shallows at night; juveniles and adolescents more often in shallows during day. Solitary but may aggregate around food sources. Litter size 10 to 82.

12. Whitetip reef shark (*Triaenodon obesus*)
East Africa and Red Sea, east to Panama, north to southern Japan and south to Australia. Lagoons, reef flats, reef faces and slopes, 0 to 40 meters (0 to 130 feet) deep. Solitary or in aggregations. Litter size 1 to 5.

13. Zebra shark (*Stegostoma varium*)
East Africa and Red Sea, east to Samoa, north to Japan and south to Australia. Lagoons, reef channels, reef faces and slopes, 1 to 70 meters (3.3 to 228 feet) deep. Solitary or in groups; forms breeding aggregations. Lays 7 eggs at a time at intervals of 6 to 8 days.

LEFT: A great hammerhead shark (*Sphyrna mokarran*) swims over a coral reef in the Bahamas. This shark commonly hunts in habitats adjacent to the coral reef, such as the bordering sand flats and slopes. Here the great hammerhead searches for one of its favorite foods, stingrays. These sharks have been observed pursuing and pinning rays to the bottom using the front edge of their head. But, as their name implies, stingrays use their barbed stingers for defense, and stingray stingers are often found in and around the mouth and in the throat of great hammerheads. One shark had 96 stingers embedded in its throat and did not appear to be bothered by them. While stingrays are a favored food, great hammerheads also eat other elasmobranchs, including small sharks and guitarfishes, as well as bony fishes and squid. While it is often found in nearshore habitats, the great hammerhead will also ply the open ocean.

ABOVE: Carpetsharks, or wobbegongs are found in the shallow waters of the tropical and temperate Western Pacific and eastern Indian Ocean, but are most common on coral reefs off Australia and New Guinea. There are 12 species of carpetsharks in the family Orectolobidae. The tasseled wobbegong (*Eucrossorhinus dasypogon*), pictured here, has an elaborate beard of skin appendages on its chin that extends from pectoral fin to pectoral fin. These dermal lobes are branched and resemble the corals in the lower left of the picture. Their coral-like shape and coloration breaks up their silhouette and allows them to blend into the reef, rendering them very difficult to see when they rest on the bottom. Consequently they are superb ambush hunters.

A frequent visitor to coral reefs is the sleek common blacktip shark (*Carcharhinus limbatus*). Blacktips are found around the world in tropical and subtropical waters, generally occurring in coastal and shelf habitats, though also around oceanic islands. The common blacktip uses shallow bays and estuaries as nursery grounds. The juvenile sharks aggregate at specific locations during the day and disperse at night, when they hunt for crustaceans, squid and small fishes. Juvenile and adolescent blacktips often form mixed schools with similar-sized sharks such as blacknose and sandbar sharks (*Carcharhinus acronotus* and *C. plumbeus*). Like salmon, the young sharks will return to their breeding areas when it is time for them to give birth to their own pups — a phenomenon known as natal philopatry.

This shark, and the closely related spinner shark (*Carcharhinus brevipinna*), is known to breach out of the water, reaching heights of at least 2 meters (7 feet) and spinning around its axis as many as three or four times. This is believed to be part of a foraging behavior, in which the sharks rush vertically through a school of fish near the surface and are launched out of the water by their own momentum. When large groups of blacktips, sometimes numbering 100 or more individuals, feed on schools of mullet, many of these sharks leap from the water synchronously during the foraging melee.

Open Ocean

The silky shark (*Carcharhinus falciformis*) is a wide-ranging species, most often found in the pelagic (open ocean) environment. In some areas they occur coastally. Juveniles are particularly common in nearshore nursery areas but are also found in the open ocean associating with floating debris. Normally found at depths of less than 200 meters (600 feet), they can bounce down to at least 500 meters (1,650 feet), possibly on hunting forays. Aggregating in large numbers, they are vulnerable to capture by fisheries. Their populations have dropped sharply over the past decade due to overfishing, often as bycatch in tuna fisheries, particularly purse-seine fisheries, a result of their predilection for following tuna schools. They rank among the top most valuable species in the shark fin trade.

The world's largest commute takes place in the open ocean, and many sharks have evolved to feed on the commuters. At dusk, throughout Earth's oceans, heavy traffic moves vertically from the depths up to the warm, productive surface layer. Just before dawn, all lanes are heading back down. This daily routine, known as diel vertical migration, is initiated by the smallest zooplankton, which hide in the dark depths during the day and graze near the surface under the cover of night.

Animals of every link in the food chain join the commuting masses, including mysid shrimp, crab larvae, lanternfish, squid and swordfish, all the way up to the ocean's largest predatory fish, the white shark. The name of the game in this moving community is "eat and don't get eaten." But with no hiding structures in the open blue water, darkness provides the best refuge for the tiny animals. This is why they rest in the cool, dark depths, just beyond the sun's penetrating reach, during the day and why rush hour occurs precisely at dawn and dusk. The result is a coordinated movement of thick, living soup, a blanket of animals known as the "deep scattering layer." This layer is a rich feeding ground for sharks that track the commute, such as threshers, porbeagles and makos, as well as cookie-cutters, lantern sharks and the plankton-eating giants, whale, basking and megamouth sharks.

The common thresher shark (*Alopias vulpinus*) is found throughout the world's tropical and temperate seas. The obvious characteristic that defines thresher sharks is the extremely large upper lobe of the caudal fin. The shark uses this elongated lobe to strike and stun fish, after which it circles around and consumes them. In order to observe this behavior more closely, scientists towed live chub mackerel behind a boat and filmed the behavior of thresher sharks attracted to the bait. The rate of thresher strike success was very high, about 65 percent. The threshers did not always strike the prey with the tip of the tail but used other portions of the caudal fin as well; the tail strikes are extremely fast, lasting on average 237 milliseconds. The common thresher prefers small schooling fishes such as anchovies, sardines and mackerel — perfect targets for its caudal whip.

Under the Ice

Sharks have successfully colonized virtually every ocean environment, including the polar seas. The high-latitude regions of the ocean are seasonally very productive, but the frigid temperatures require special adaptations. Sharks have taken two very different approaches to dealing with this frigid environment. They fight the cold either by heating their body or by allowing their body to cool but preventing its cells from icing.

The Greenland shark (*Somniosus microcephalus*) at times lives under arctic sea ice, where the water temperature remains below 0°C (32°F). To protect protein function and avoid ice crystal formation in its body, it maintains high levels of a chemical called trimethylamine oxide, which along with the shark's high urea concentration acts as a natural antifreeze. The levels of trimethylamine oxide are so high in Greenland sharks that their flesh is toxic, and unless cured for months, it can be fatal if consumed. Although lethargic, they have a voracious and diverse appetite, consuming prey from snails and sea stars to narwhals and even caribou.

Salmon sharks (*Lamna ditropis*) can overwinter in the Gulf of Alaska and in the Bering Sea, where they experience near freezing temperatures around 2°C (35.5°F). In contrast with Greenland sharks they are not lethargic but are highly active predators with a fast metabolism. Salmon sharks retain the heat they generate from digestion and activity to maintain a core body temperature near 26°C (79°F), despite the icy waters they inhabit. Maintaining this higher temperature means that the locomotor muscles function like those of mammals. These muscles are what power continuous swimming in sharks, and they enable the salmon shark to sustain powerful, high-energy swimming not possible for an ectothermic fish in these cold waters.

Reaching lengths up to 5.5 meters (18 feet) or more, the Greenland shark (*Somniosus microcephalus*) is one of the largest species of sharks and is the largest species of fish in polar waters. It occurs in the North Atlantic, ranging from the Arctic Ocean to the southeastern United States in the Western Atlantic and to France in the Eastern Atlantic. It is the shark with the broadest known depth distribution, ranging from the surface down to 3,000 meters (9,900 feet), generally occurring at greater depths in the more southern part of its range. To catch this species, the Inuit drip blood into a hole cut through the ice; when a shark appears at the hole, they harpoon it or simply grab it and drag it out of the water.

The Greenland shark is typically thought of as being a particularly lethargic and sluggish shark, which is reflected in its genus name *Somniosus,* which is Latin for "sleepy." This reputation has been challenged, however, as the species is known to consume large and active prey that include dolphins, halibut and even caribou, suggesting that it may be more active than observations imply. That said, studies have shown that individuals living under the ice are some of the slowest fishes of their size on record, and scientists believe there is no way that an arctic Greenland shark could catch a wary seal, a prey type known to be on this shark's bill of fare. So how do they catch pinnipeds? They may have another carnivore to thank. It turns out that in the Arctic, seals sleep under the ice to avoid polar bears; thus it is possible that these languid sharks sneak up on seals as they slumber. Greenland sharks are also important scavengers of whale carcasses, tearing open dead cetaceans that have sunk to the seafloor, allowing other scavengers to gain access to the nutritious blubber and innards.

The Greenland shark plays host to a parasitic copepod that attaches itself to the cornea of its eyes, causing lesions that impair vision and may even cause blindness. This infection is quite common in individuals from the Arctic. In one study, only 1 percent of sharks did not carry this parasite. The nature of the relationship is unclear, though it has been speculated that the copepod, which is light-colored and possibly luminescent, may serve as a lure that draws in prey to the hunting shark. It is believed that the decrease in visual acuity does not harm the shark; Greenland sharks remain effective hunters, living as they do in low light conditions where vision is likely less important than other senses such as smell and electroreception.

A population of Greenland sharks that enter the mouth of the St. Lawrence River in Quebec is not afflicted by these copepods, and as a result they do not suffer from impaired vision. It is well-known that submersion in less saline waters kills marine copepods, so parasite removal may be one explanation for their incursion into brackish water.

Fresh Water

Large bull sharks living in Lake Nicaragua were once thought to be landlocked freshwater creatures — until they were seen swimming up the river rapids. Their landlocked status was debunked when scientists finally tracked their journey along the entire length of the Rio San Juan, which connects Lake Nicaragua with the Caribbean Sea.

There are no known sharks and only a handful of ray species considered true freshwater species. Still, a number of sharks (some 5 percent of elasmobranchs) make extensive use of freshwater habitats, mostly the world's major river systems. Bull sharks have been observed in the Zambezi River, 2,500 kilometers (200 miles) up the Amazon River and as far up the Mississippi as Illinois. Another rare and poorly known group of sharks that utilize fresh water are the so-called river sharks of the genus *Glyphis*. River sharks, like bull sharks, are members of the family Carcharhinidae. While there is still considerable uncertainty about their taxonomy, the six species currently known in this genus are found in coastal and riverine habitats in the Indo-Pacific region. All are critically endangered.

There are plenty of freshwater fish, so why not freshwater sharks? Sharks face a major challenge in fresh water because they have a different mechanism for maintaining the saltiness, or osmolarity, of their blood and tissue. Teleost fish get their fluids by drinking water, then excreting excess salt through their gills. Sharks do not drink water. Instead their tissues are "saltier" than seawater, and that difference forces water to flow directly into their tissues through their skin. This works well in salt water, but the difference becomes too extreme in fresh water and is very energetically costly to adjust to.

LEFT: Bull sharks (*Carcharhinus leucas*) are one of a handful of shark species capable of moving between freshwater and saltwater habitats.

RIGHT: The distribution of bull sharks changes as they grow and mature. Newborn and juvenile bull sharks commonly reside in freshwater or brackish water habitats such as rivers, estuaries or lagoons and they move to coastal marine habitats as they grow larger and reach maturity. Pregnant females then return to their original habitats, where they give birth. The bull shark is a powerful top predator in coastal habitats in subtropical and tropical seas. These sharks are highly opportunistic foragers and are well-known to consume large prey such as dolphins, sea turtles and other species of elasmobranchs. They are believed to be an important predator on other species of sharks, especially juveniles and smaller species. Larger bull sharks are also known to eat smaller individuals of their own species, which may be a factor in why bull sharks segregate by size, with smaller sharks living in different habitats than larger ones. Gravid and postpartum females do not feed until they leave the nursery area, an adaptation that helps reduce filial cannibalism.

Low-Oxygen Environments

An epaulette shark (*Hemiscyllium ocellatum*) works the shallow inner reef habitat close to shore. Rather than swim, epaulette sharks tend to "crawl" around on their paired fins, sometimes in the intertidal zone in water barely deep enough to cover their backs, accessing habitat relatively free from competing predators.

Sharks can "drown" in water if it is low in dissolved oxygen; they are thereby excluded from low-oxygen (hypoxic) habitats if they cannot get enough oxygen to sustain their activity. The epaulette shark (*Hemiscyllium ocellatum*) is a rare exception in its ability to withstand periodic hypoxia and even several hours completely without oxygen (anoxia). The shallow reef pools of the Great Barrier Reef, where the epaulette shark lives, often get cut off from the open ocean as the tide goes out. The dissolved oxygen in the pools is quickly used up by corals, algae and other small animals attached to the reef. The plummeting oxygen levels during low tide would be fatal to most predators. To cope, epaulette sharks increase the blood circulation between heart and brain. They reduce nonessential brain functions, allowing just enough metabolic activity to prevent neuron death while still remaining alert to their environment. Their regular exposure to low oxygen with each tidal cycle is like an athletic training regime; it serves to precondition the shark for the next hypoxic event. Its adaptation to low oxygen enables the epaulette shark to exploit shallow reef habitats, feeding on worms and crabs while relatively free from competition.

A much larger shark, the scalloped hammerhead (*Sphyrna lewini*), is able to venture down into hypoxic depths, in a part of the tropical Eastern Pacific that is 250 to 1,000 meters (825 to 3,300 feet) deep. Known as the oxygen minimum layer, this region is off-limits for other large predators such as marlins, sailfish and tunas. It is still unknown whether the hammerhead shark uses a technique similar to that of the epaulette shark to deal with the low oxygen levels in this zone.

A scalloped hammerhead shark (*Sphyrna lewini*) glides through the darkness. Few large, active predators are able to venture into the deep low-oxygen areas that occur naturally in certain regions of the world's oceans. The scalloped hammerhead shark stands apart. It may dive down to pursue prey such as the jumbo squid that is believed to take refuge in the oxygen minimum zone, where most large predators are unable to penetrate.

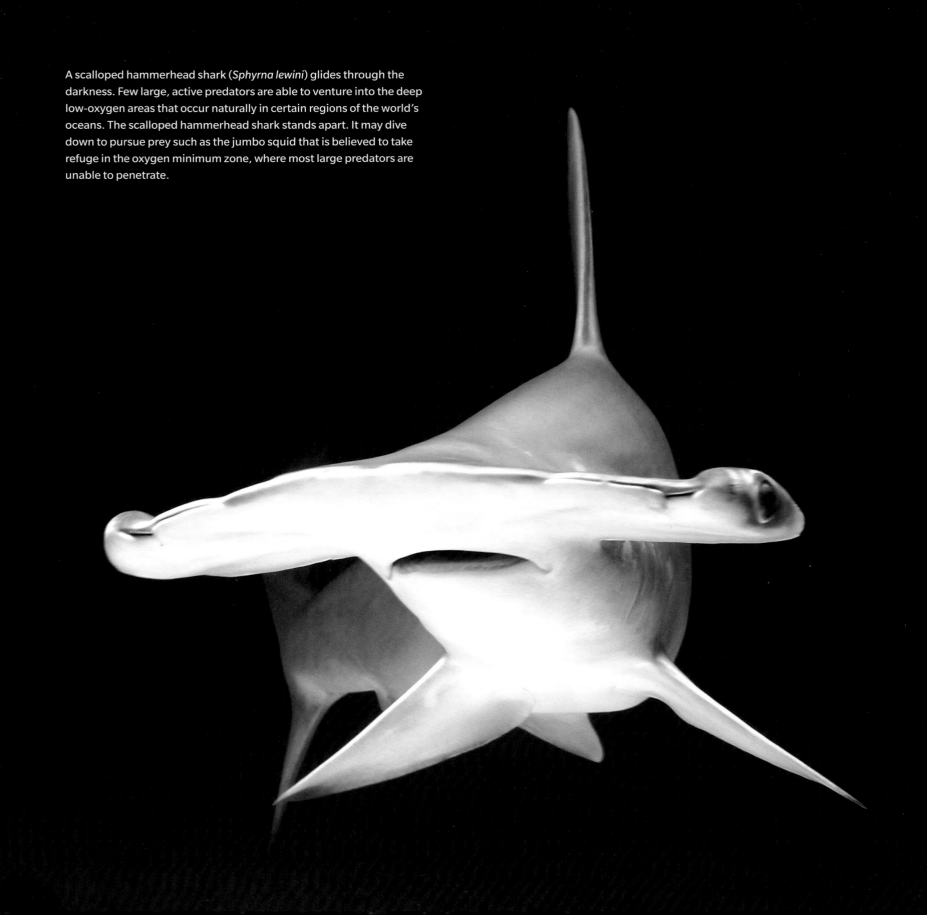

The Milne Bay epaulette shark (*Hemiscyllium michaeli*) is a recently described species from shallow reefs off Papua New Guinea. It is a nocturnal shark that spends its days tucked away in reef crevices, from which it emerges at night to hunt invertebrate prey.

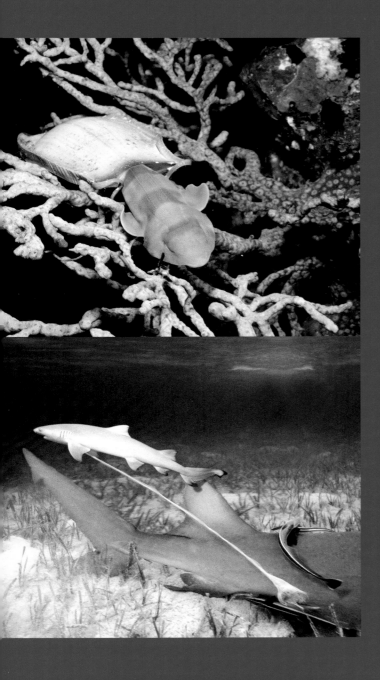

2
Life Histories

A key ecological role of any predator is keeping prey populations in check. When predators are removed, prey populations can increase too sharply and deplete their own food sources. But what keeps sharks in check at the top? Many have few or no predators at all. A top predator population, unchecked, can also overwhelm its prey, leading to a crash in both populations. Sharks, however, have a number of unique traits that make for low population productivity, traits that may keep shark numbers from increasing too rapidly. They mature late, have lengthy gestation periods and produce few offspring compared with other fishes. This slow-and-steady population growth strategy may be one key to sharks' sustained success as top predators — a mechanism for self-regulation that keeps their own population numbers in check.

Although the sharks' strategy has proved a winner for some 400 million years, it is also a double-edged sword: risk of extinction is strongly dependent on such life-history traits. Animals with low productivity are less able to compensate if there is a catastrophic decrease in their population; therefore they can be more vulnerable to extinction. In the absence of significant natural predators, this is generally not a problem. But if a new predator suddenly became a threat, sharks would be left holding the wrong cards.

Slow population growth and reproduction are just one facet of the strategy. The flipside is that the few offspring sharks do produce are large, well-developed and ready to fend for themselves as soon as they are born. To produce these youngsters, sharks use a range of strange and fascinating reproductive pathways. Given the high parental investment, these few but strong young sharks have enhanced chances for survival compared with other newborn sea creatures. In this way a slow but reliable stream of toothy new recruits becomes the next generation of ocean predators.

While developing inside the egg, shark embryos such as these white-spotted bamboo sharks (*Chiloscyllium plagiosum*) live a remarkably active life. During the later stages, enzymes are released that open up small holes in the corners of the egg case, allowing outside water to circulate through the case and replenish its oxygen supply. The embryo pumps water through the egg case by using its tail, in addition to actively pumping water over its gills.

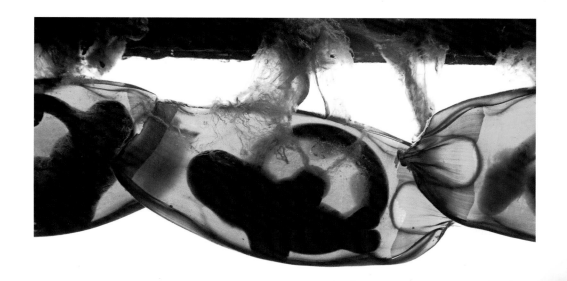

Female spiny dogfish (*Squalus acanthias*) give birth to young sharks that have been nourished by an external yolk sac (aplacental viviparity). The embryos subsist on this yolk sac as they grow and develop inside the mother. Several weeks prior to birth, its remaining contents are moved to an internal yolk sac, which will support the pups following birth while they search for their first meal.

A pregnant female tiger shark (*Galeocerdo cuvier*) patrols a reef. The largest requiem shark (family Carcharhinidae), the tiger shark has a slow reproductive cycle. Females give birth only once every three years, to a litter ranging in size from 3 to 57 pups. In addition, after mating, females can store sperm for as long as four to five months before using it to fertilize their eggs.

Life History Strategies

Few, Large Offspring

Most fishes spawn. That is, females release thousands of eggs directly into the water and male sperm washes over the eggs to fertilize them. From these thousands of tiny developing embryos only a small fraction are expected to survive. Sharks are much more like mammals, in that they give birth to a small number of large offspring with a comparatively high chance of survival. Sharks are fertilized internally and gestate for months, or even years. By the time the pups are born — or hatch, in the case of the few egg-laying species — they are large and ready to fend for themselves.

Shark litter sizes vary considerably, from the sand tiger shark (*Carcharias taurus*), which averages only one or two pups, to the blue shark, which can have up to 134 at a time, although on average the number is around 30. The whale shark is the most fecund, giving birth to as many as 300 pups at once that measure 40 to 60 centimeters (16 to 23 inches). Being born large increases an animal's chances for survival, but producing large offspring takes longer and requires a greater energy investment from the maternal parent.

Emerging from its egg case, a newly born blotchy swell shark (*Cephaloscyllium umbratile*) is ready to swim, hide and hunt. Blotchy swell sharks are members of the catshark family Scyliorhinidae. They deposit eggs in pairs, which take about a year to hatch. After hatching, the young sharks seek shelter in reef crevices to avoid predators. They are nourished by yolk that remains in the stomach; after that is exhausted, they hunt small invertebrates that share their diurnal haunts or move into the open to hunt at night. Because they are smaller at hatching, swell shark pups are potential prey for a number of bony fishes such as scorpionfishes and groupers, as well as other rocky reef–dwelling sharks, including the Japanese wobbegong (*Orectolobus japonicus*).

A sand tiger shark (*Carcharias taurus*) swims languidly by, surrounded by baitfish that seem to know the safest place to be. Sand tiger sharks "put all their eggs in one basket," producing only one pup per ovary. But after a nine-month gestation period, at birth the pups, around 1 meter (3.3 feet) in length, are already formidable predators.

A newborn lemon shark (*Negaprion brevirostris*) makes its first swimming tail-beats. Lemon sharks give birth to between four and seven pups every other year. At birth the neonates are immediately ready to pursue their own prey and to avoid being captured themselves. Remoras that hitch a ride on and clean the mother shark of parasites also dine on the afterbirth during the delivery process.

Late Maturity

Although sharks are born large, they are late bloomers. In order to have large offspring, female sharks must first attain a large size themselves. Therefore more energy is channeled toward growth, and the onset of reproduction is delayed. In the deep ocean, conditions are cold and dark and growth is slowed down considerably. As a result, deepwater sharks are particularly late to mature. On average, these deepwater predators begin reproducing only at around 13 years of age. The spiny dogfish, the shark species most targeted by commercial fisheries, begins producing offspring only after 17 years of age. Another deepwater shark, the leafscale gulper shark (*Centrophorus squamosus*), reaches reproductive maturity only by age 35 — more than two and a half times later than humans. Oceanic pelagic sharks such as the oceanic whitetip (*Carcharhinus longimanus*) become mature by 11 years of age, on average.

The leafscale gulper shark (*Centrophorus squamosus*) is a deepwater shark that is commonly caught in deepwater fisheries in Europe. Deep-sea sharks are generally late in maturing and have few young, so they are incredibly sensitive to fishing pressure. A close relative of the leafscale gulper shark, the gulper shark (*C. granulosus*), matures between 12 and 16 years of age, produces one pup per litter and has a two-year gestation, with occasional resting periods between litters. As a result, this species has the lowest reproductive potential of any elasmobranch, with an estimated lifetime reproductive output of only 12 pups. (Photo courtesy of ©OceanLab, University of Aberdeen)

Lengthy Gestation

Being born large has advantages for sharks, which must fend for themselves from the moment they are born. But attaining a large size at birth takes time and energetic investment by the mother. Interestingly, shark species with greater maternal investment also generally develop larger brains. This is particularly true for smaller species, in which extra provisioning by the mother may literally provide a head start to help them survive the early years on their own.

Many shark species have extended gestation periods, often exceeding one year. Consequently, females cannot participate in the mating and pupping season every year. The frilled shark (*Chlamydoselachus anguineus*) has a gestation period of 3.5 years or more, the longest known for any vertebrate and almost twice as long as the longest gestation in a land mammal — the African elephant, at just under two years.

The frilled shark has no distinct breeding season, a common trait among sharks in the deep sea, where there is virtually no sunlight to mark the change of seasons. This rare "living fossil" is one of only six species in its order, Hexanchiformes. The frilled shark's primitive appearance and undulating, eel-like motion are believed to be linked to reported sightings of sea serpents.

Reproductive Strategies

Ovipary

The majority of shark species give birth to live pups, a mode known as vivipar-ity. However, a number of species have transitioned to becoming egg-layers, or oviparous, including bullhead sharks, catsharks and some carpetsharks. Inter-estingly, this transition to ovipary among the modern sharks occurred indepen-dently at least half a dozen times. Oviparous sharks are all bottom-dwelling, or benthic, species. They produce leathery and structurally intricate egg cases that are sometimes called "mermaid's purses." The sharks deposit these cases, anchored near the seafloor, and then leave. The developing shark babies are on their own and must begin feeding for themselves as soon as they hatch.

Vivipary

Most shark species today still share the original reproductive mode of vivipary, in which the developing embryo is nourished solely by a yolk-filled sac that is attached to it via a short egg stalk. However, a general evolutionary transition has been toward modes in which the mother provides additional nutrition to the embryo, and this occurs in a variety of strange ways. Some of the higher, more recently evolved species of Carcharhiniformes have adapted a placental development mode similar to that of mammals, in which the yolk stalk is elon-gated, forming an umbilical cord attached to the mother through which the embryo receives yolk stores from the parent during initial development.

When depositing eggs, female oviparous (egg-laying) sharks carefully select a suitable location; they may return to the same place to lay year after year. Some egg cases, such as those of the swell shark (*Cephaloscyllium ventriosum*) (in photo top right), have long, coiled tendrils that extend from the corners of the case. When laying her eggs, the female coils these tendrils around suitable structures such as rocks, seaweeds or corals; the tendrils secure the egg case in place. The egg cases of the oviparous carpetsharks are purse-shaped, with hairlike fibers that anchor them to seafloor structures, while those of horn sharks (*Heterodontus* species) (in photo bottom right) have a more conical shape, with spiral flanges running down the length of the case. It is thought that the female horn shark may pick up the egg case in her mouth and insert it into a crevice, where the spiral flange holds the case in place.

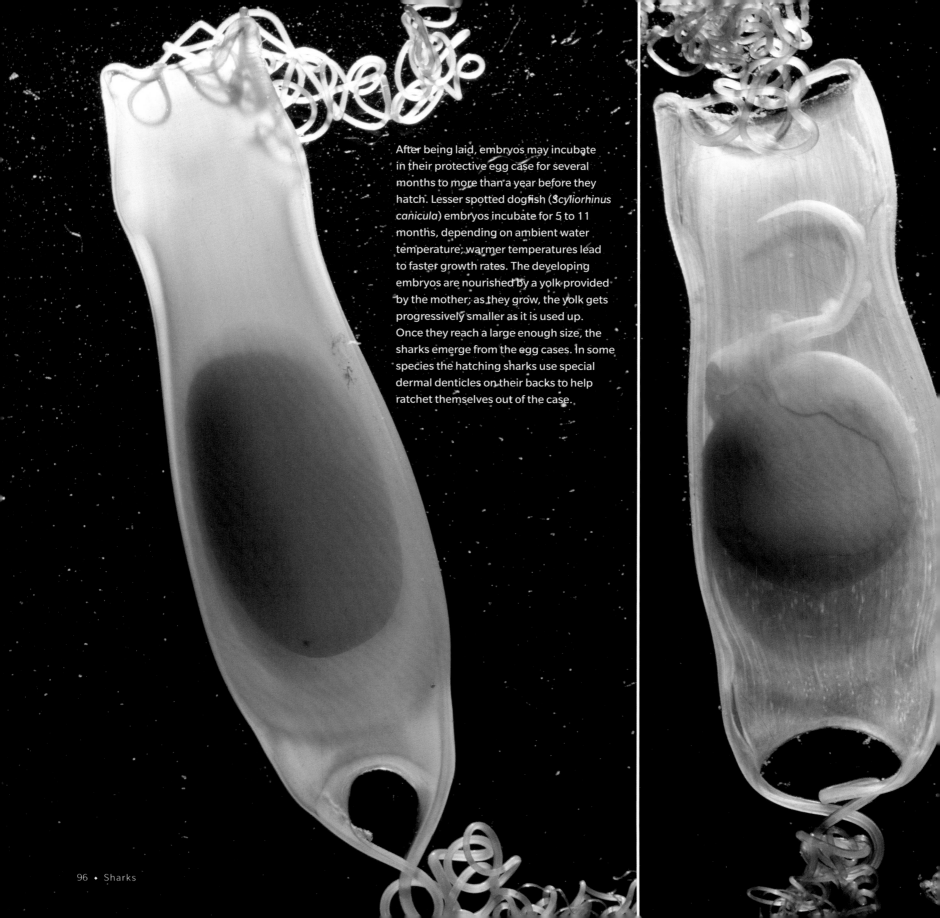

After being laid, embryos may incubate in their protective egg case for several months to more than a year before they hatch. Lesser spotted dogfish (*Scyliorhinus canicula*) embryos incubate for 5 to 11 months, depending on ambient water temperature; warmer temperatures lead to faster growth rates. The developing embryos are nourished by a yolk provided by the mother; as they grow, the yolk gets progressively smaller as it is used up. Once they reach a large enough size, the sharks emerge from the egg cases. In some species the hatching sharks use special dermal denticles on their backs to help ratchet themselves out of the case.

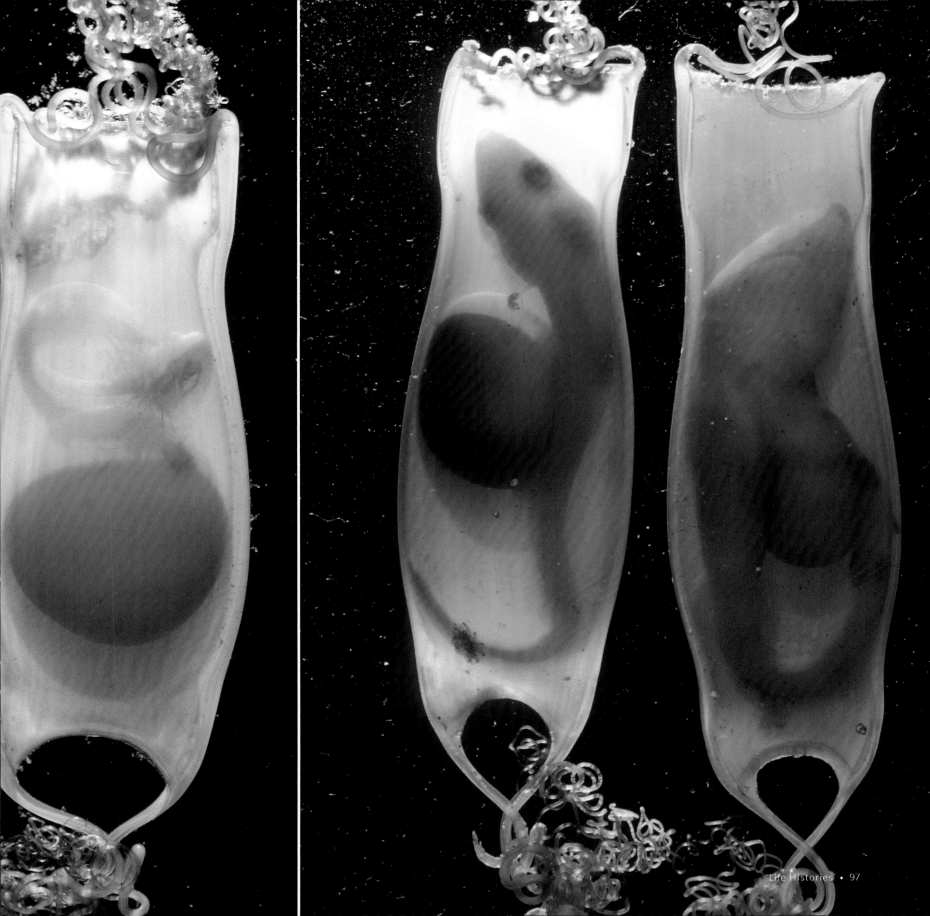

Embryonic whiskery sharks (*Furgaleus macki*) with external yolk sacs. Once the yolk sac is absorbed and the shark is born, for a period of time there remains a scar where the yolk stalk attached to the abdomen of the young shark — in effect, the baby shark has a belly button. Researchers use this feature to identify newly born sharks. The whiskery shark practices aplacental vivipary.

Oophagy

The porbeagle shark (*Lamna nasus*) is a close relative of the mako and has a similar reproductive life history — both are oophagous. Porbeagles occur in the colder waters of the Northern and Southern Hemispheres. In the western North Atlantic they reside primarily in the waters off Canada. However, until recently, where these large sharks gave birth remained a mystery. Satellite tagging research has now shown that pregnant females move as far as 2,345 kilometers (1,450 miles) south — to the Sargasso Sea — to give birth in warm waters far to the south of their known distribution.

In some shark species the developing embryos seemingly take matters of nourishment into their own hands: they begin eating before leaving the womb. In addition to their egg sac, oophagous, or egg-eating, embryos consume additional, unfertilized eggs produced by the mother throughout most of the pregnancy. Oophagy has evolved twice, in the Lamniformes (all 11 families) and in the small Carcharhiniformes family Pseudotriakidae, the false catsharks.

Intrauterine Cannibalism

The most extreme form of oophagy is intrauterine cannibalism, or adelphophagy, in which developing siblings are consumed, usually by the first embryo that develops. Adelphophagy is known to occur only in the sand tiger shark (*Carcharias taurus*). By the time sand tigers are born, after a 9-to-12-month pregnancy, only a single, large cannibal emerges from the uterus.

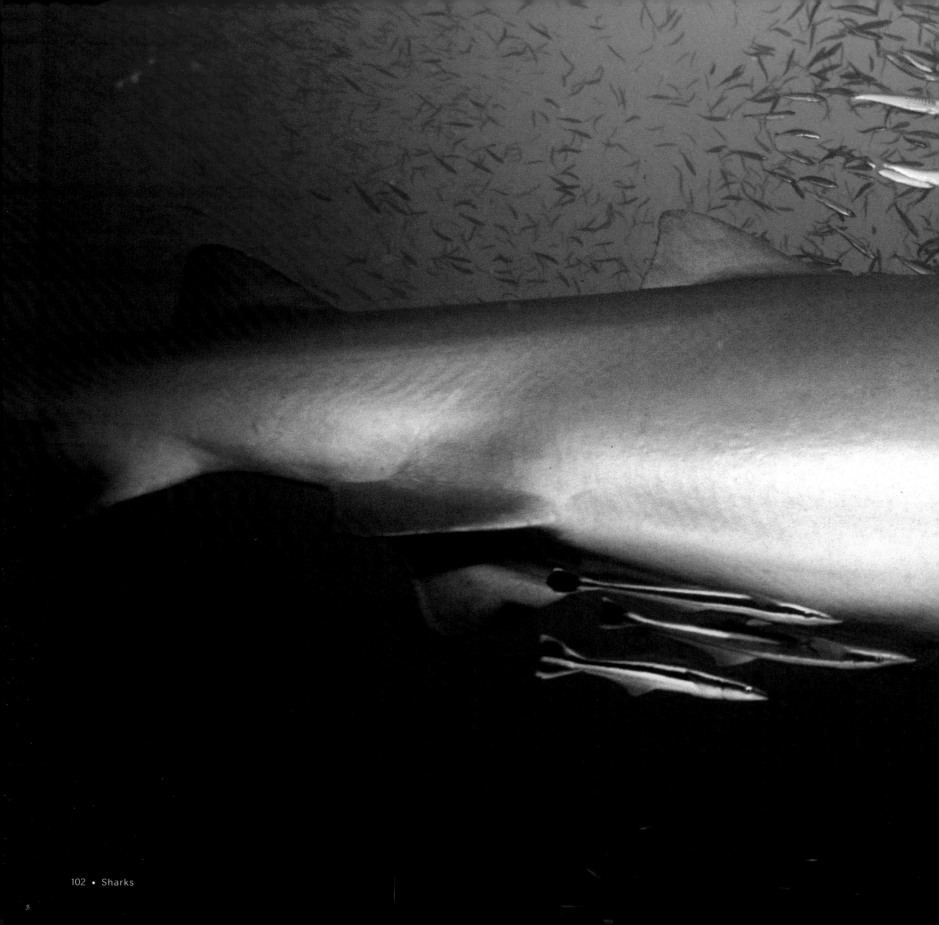

Extreme sibling rivalry — they literally eat each other — is likely occurring inside this gravid female sand tiger shark (*Carcharias taurus*) as she hovers nearly motionless in a school of baitfish. The ability to hover in the water is a very unusual for a shark; they generally either need to keep moving forward so their pectoral fins can generate lift (like the wings of an airplane) or rest on the bottom. Sand tiger sharks developed a novel way to get around this. They swim to the surface, stick their head out of the water and gulp air. The air is then forced into the stomach, where it provides the buoyancy needed to hover motionless.

Shortfin mako sharks (*Isurus oxyrinchus*) are highly active and have an elevated metabolism, requiring an accelerated feeding rate. Like most other sharks, mako embryos subsist on an external yolk sac. However, once they have used up this initial supply of yolk, the pregnant female produces huge numbers of unfertilized eggs for the embryos to consume. The tiny makos, between 4 and 18 in a litter, actively feed on these eggs while in the womb.

Early Life

Unlike most mammals and birds, there is no parental care for sharks. It's "good-bye and good luck" when they are born or the eggs are laid. To avoid predation or even parental cannibalism, sharks generally give birth in specific areas known as pupping grounds. And once born, neonate sharks generally live in designated places known as nursery areas. These areas tend to be in shallow, productive coastal regions where young sharks can find some refuge and plenty to eat. Nursery areas include important coastal environments such as bays, mangrove swamps, coastal lagoons and even rivers. The same pupping grounds and nursery areas are used year after year, becoming seasonally crowded with young developing sharks.

OPPOSITE PAGE: Juvenile blacktip reef sharks (*Carcharhinus melanopterus*) use very shallow sand-flat habitats as nursery areas, presumably for protection from larger blacktip reef sharks, grey reef sharks and tiger sharks. The blacktip reef shark is ubiquitous on coral reefs in the Indo-Pacific region. The adults tend to inhabit shallower depths than other requiem sharks in the coral reef community and live in a limited home range. The blacktip reef shark does most of its hunting at night, although, like most sharks, it is an opportunist. It is a fast swimmer that will chase down reef fishes and stingrays and attack assemblages of surgeonfishes as they spawn. Groups of blacktip reef sharks will also drive and trap schools of mullet along the shoreline before launching a feeding assault. There are even reports of these sharks chasing schooling fish into shore, sliding up onto the beach and wiggling back into the water after attempting to capture their stranded quarry.

ABOVE: A juvenile lemon shark (*Negaprion brevirostris*) swims through a mangrove forest nursery area in the Bahamas. These shallow habitats provide shelter from larger predators while providing young sharks with abundant prey to feed upon. As they grow larger and become less likely to be consumed by other predators, their home range gets progressively larger. During the transition to the deeper adult habitat, the ability of their eyes to detect light changes as well. The visual pigment in the eyes of juveniles is optimized to function in a shallow-water environment, whereas the light sensitivity of the visual pigment in adult eyes is shifted to better detect light in deeper, bluer water.

Mating Strategies

Mating Organs

Unlike with the vast majority of bony fishes, fertilization in sharks is internal. Males transfer sperm into the female's oviducts with the aid of two organs called claspers. These are modifications of the inner edges of the male's pelvic fins and are analogous to the mammalian penis. During most mating events, only one clasper is inserted at a time. So why do sharks have two? It has been suggested that they have an extra sex organ in case an unreceptive female bites one off. However, it is more likely a case of convenience — having a pair means it is easier for the male to successfully insert a clasper no matter which side it approaches its potential mate from.

In male sharks a pair of siphon sacs (located on the abdomen just under the skin) are connected to the claspers by way of small openings. These sacs are filled with seawater prior to mating, possibly by repeated flexing of the clasper or by swimming with the clasper rotated forward. Water, copious secretions from the sac (including serotonin, a smooth-muscle contractant) and semen are injected into the female's reproductive tract during mating. This fluid helps lubricate the claspers, provides a medium for increasing sperm viability and may help wash away seminal fluid deposited by other males.

Mating Behavior

While variations exist in shark mating behaviors, some patterns are seen in most species studied thus far. Courtship usually begins with the male closely following the female, often with his nose near her cloaca. Females probably emit pheromones that attract and possibly inform suitors about their reproductive state.

All sharks and rays whose love lives have been observed engage in biting. Males bite their potential mates, sometimes inflicting very violent "love nips" that can leave deep wounds and permanent scarring. This fact was well-known to fisherman who used to exploit the hides of sharks to make shoes, belts and other sharkskin goods. The skin of female sharks was often rejected because of the scars caused by males' biting behavior. Male biting may serve to stimulate ovulation or sexual receptivity in females. In some species it may also enable the male to maintain contact with a struggling female during copulation. Males may grip the female's gill region in their mouth or ingest her pectoral fin and

hold on tightly. To facilitate this love grip, the teeth of male sharks of some species are more elongate and slenderer than those of the female.

When it comes to sex positions, sharks employ several, depending on the species in question. Most lie or swim alongside each other with the male's posterior body region curled under that of the female; this is seen in whitetip reef sharks, epaulette and bamboo sharks, wobbegongs and lemon sharks. A few species, such as the blacktip reef shark, mate belly to belly. In the more supple-bodied catsharks, the male coils around the female while they lie on the seafloor.

Mating can take a toll on female sharks. Whereas males may continue to mate again as long as their energy stores allow, females can mate only very briefly — enough to acquire sufficient sperm from fit males. Further courtship becomes too costly in terms of injury, and males may be avoided, resulting in segregation of the sexes.

Sexual segregation has already been noted in some 40 species of sharks and is thought to be a general characteristic in elasmobranchs. For instance, male white sharks leave seal rookeries off the coast of California each spring to head for an area halfway out to Hawaii known as the "White Shark Café." Females leaving the coast tend to wander more broadly offshore as far as Hawaii, and only briefly

Two are better than one. Instead of a penis, male sharks have a pair of claspers. These are extensions of their paired pelvic fins. Having two claspers allows sharks to be ambidextrous when it comes to courtship, ensuring success whether grasping the left or right side of the female. Once the male has firmly grasped the female and is ready to copulate, he will rotate the corresponding clasper and insert it into the female's cloaca for internal fertilization.

The shark mating game is not always easy to play. Females are often resistant to male advances. In the photo seen above, a male Port Jackson shark (*Heterodontus portusjacksoni*) holds the pectoral fin of a female and has succeeded in turning her over, but he has not been successful at inserting a clasper. In many cases the female will struggle until she breaks free of the amorous would-be partner before he has completed the act of mating.

visit the Café. One hypothesis that could explain this segregation in white sharks is an underlying mating system in which males gather in a known mating ground where females visit briefly when they are ready to be courted. Intricate mating assemblages have been noted in coastal sharks that are easier to observe.

In nurse shark mating assemblages, there are three groups of females. The first group is the "non-attracting" females; these individuals rest in the breeding area and are not courted by males. The second group is classified as "attracting but non-cooperative"; these females retreat into shallow water when approached by males and try to resist any that attempt to copulate with them. The final group is the "attracting cooperating females," which are receptive to male advances, remaining in deeper water and allowing the males to follow and eventually mate with them. Females in this group are reported to "relax" and allow the larger dominant males to grasp their fin and mate with them. Observations of these sharks, as well as those made of ray mating groups, suggest that the females do some selecting.

In many species the females copulate with more than one male during the mating season. DNA analysis of bluntnose sevengill and lemon shark litters indicates multiple paternity — as many as seven males were found to be responsible for the young in a single litter. In contrast, similar studies of a large whale shark litter and bonnethead sharks indicate that they may mate with only a single suitor during a breeding season.

Some male bony fishes are well-known for employing alternative strategies to inseminate females. Subordinate males may engage in sneaking or streaking behaviors to interrupt the reproductive efforts of more successful males. The same may occur in shark and ray mating systems. It is not uncommon for one or more males to get into the act and try to "steal" a female from a male that has already latched on to his potential mate. This may prevent the initiating male shark from successfully inserting a clasper and inseminating the female, or enable a secondary male to subdue the female while she is being held by her original suitor.

Because there have been very few observations of mating sharks, especially in the wild, very little is known about their mating behavior. Nurse sharks (*Ginglymostoma cirratum*) are one of the few species whose mating behaviors have been well documented. Nurse sharks exhibit complex social interactions during mating, with males and females actively selecting and competing for potential mates. Because female nurse sharks will mate with several males, individual newborns from the same litter may have different fathers.

A female blue shark (*Prionace glauca*) exhibits courtship wounds inflicted by an amorous male. Though this seems brutal from a human perspective, extensive biting has evolved in virtually every shark species. Research has shown that the skin of female blue sharks is up to three times thicker than their male partners' — a common sexual dimorphism in sharks. This adaptation helps the shark endure the damage inflicted during mating. These wounds heal rapidly but often leave enduring scars.

ABOVE: In almost all elasmobranchs studied to date, the male will bite the female during the mating act. In many species the target of the male's grasp is the pectoral fin. He will bite the edge of the fin or, in some species, take the entire fin into his mouth. In this photograph a male epaulette shark attaches himself to a female; he will hold on to her until he has an opportunity to swing his pelvis under hers and insert a clasper.

LEFT: A school of basking sharks (*Cetorhinus maximus*) swims off the northeast coast of the United States. Basking sharks are known to gather at thermal fronts, where their microscopic zooplankton prey aggregate. When they gather, these sharks often display a variety of interesting but poorly understood social interactions. During the summer, the attention of sharks in these aggregations shifts from feeding toward romance. The males begin to exhibit a behavior called "close-following," in which they follow females, nose to tail, in what is believed to be courtship behavior. Thus the thermal fronts that aggregate their prey also serve as a meeting place where basking sharks can not only forage but also find individuals of the opposite sex.

3

Form & Function

To live and thrive in the ocean is to be faced with constant challenges. Among the fishes swimming in today's oceans can be found numerous anatomical and physiological adaptations that arose to meet such challenges as detecting and capturing food, swimming quickly or remaining suspended at a certain depth without sinking or floating. Unique qualities that gave one individual an advantage over others have been passed down by thriving parents to their lineages and inherited by millions of generations. Variations of successful forms or traits that overcame the challenges of ocean life have evolved, and they continue to evolve today.

Sharks are among the oldest lineages of fishes, yet they possess some unique traits that work very successfully in their natural environment today. For example, sharks have a different strategy for staying afloat than bony fishes (teleosts). They also have a different skeletal structure and different teeth. Every specialized trait brings with it pros and cons or tradeoffs. Continually replacing teeth are advantageous in that sharks always have sharp tools for efficiently capturing and consuming prey, but growing so many teeth costs a considerable amount of energy. Traits and tradeoffs are tested over geologic time scales, and few have been tested for as long as the elasmobranchs' have been.

One of the extraordinary examples of unique functional form in sharks is the tail of the threshers. In all three species of the genus *Alopias*, the common (*A. vulpinus*), bigeye (*A. superciliosus*) and pelagic (*A. pelagicus*) threshers (shown in the photo), the upper lobe of the tail extends to an extreme length. The function of this tail has been demonstrated by the common thresher, using underwater video analysis. The threshers use their tail like a whip, to strike their prey; once the prey is stunned, the shark then circles back to consume its prize. On rare occasions the tail may also be used to smack seabirds floating on the ocean's surface. While the long upper caudal fin might be seen as an encumbrance to rapid swimming, these sharks can accelerate fast enough to hurl themselves completely out of the water. In certain locations they engage in this behavior frequently; while the purpose is still in question, it may serve for communicating with members of its own kind or to scare schooling fish into a ball so they are easier to stun with the tail.

Skin

Toothed Skin Makes
Hydrodynamic Sense

Sharkskin looks smooth but feels like sandpaper. It gets its roughness from a covering of microscopic overlapping scales called dermal denticles. While they resemble the scales on teleost fish, the dermal denticles are actually more similar to teeth. Denticles have a hard, enamel-like finish over a layer of dentine, and a pulp cavity at the core. In addition to providing strong physical armor that protects sharks from injury, the tiny dermal denticles help them swim faster and increase their maneuverability in the water. The shape and configuration of the denticles channel water to create a cushion of micro-turbulence vortices, or swirls, next to the skin, making the shark "slippery" and more hydrodynamic. This is similar to the way a golf ball, with its tiny indentations on the surface, can travel much farther and faster than a similar ball with a smooth surface.

Skin or tooth? A close-up view of the rostrum of a horn shark (*Heterodontus francisci*) illustrates how dermal denticle scales and teeth have essentially the same structure although a different function. Interestingly, teeth evolved from dermal scales, and not the other way around. The ancient jawless fishes that predated sharks had dermal denticles called odontodes. Jaw teeth likely evolved through the gradual movement of dermal scales into the mouths of early vertebrates over thousands of generations.

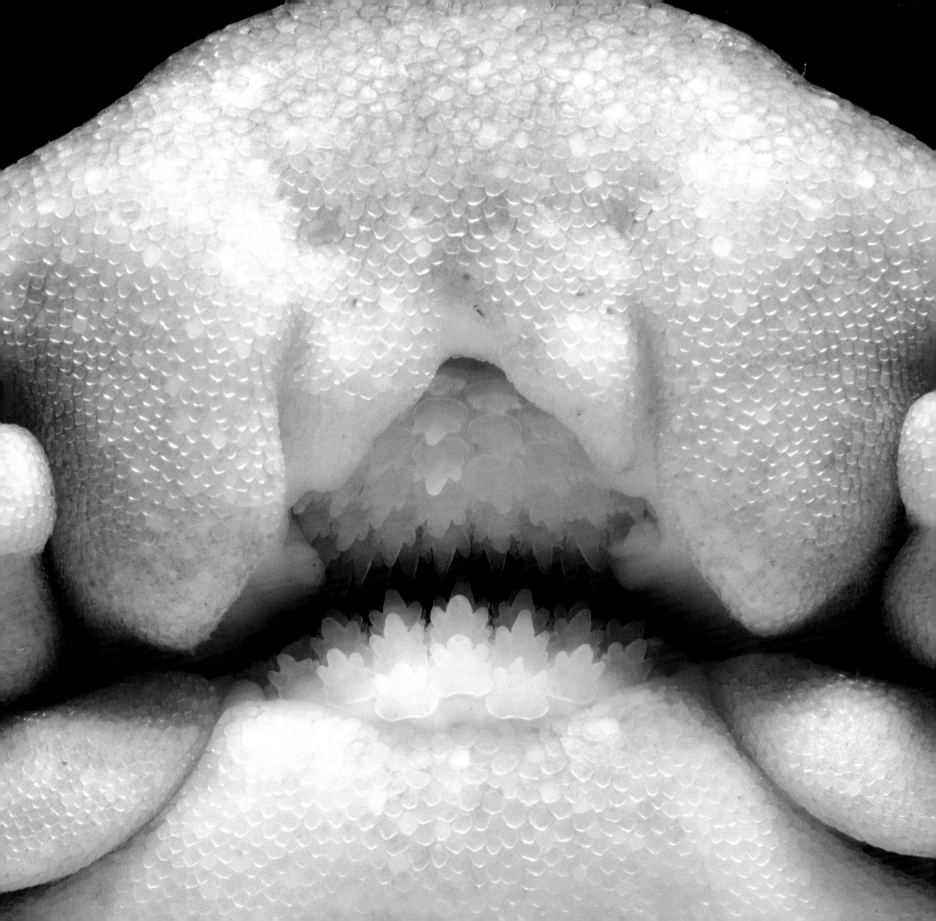

Form follows function. The shape and size of dermal denticles vary greatly by shark species, depending on the relative importance of protection versus reducing hydrodynamic drag. The dermal denticles of fast open-ocean species such as the white shark tend to be more hydrodynamic than those of bottom-dwelling or slow-moving sharks such as the velvet belly lantern shark. The shape of dermal denticles also varies based on location on the body.

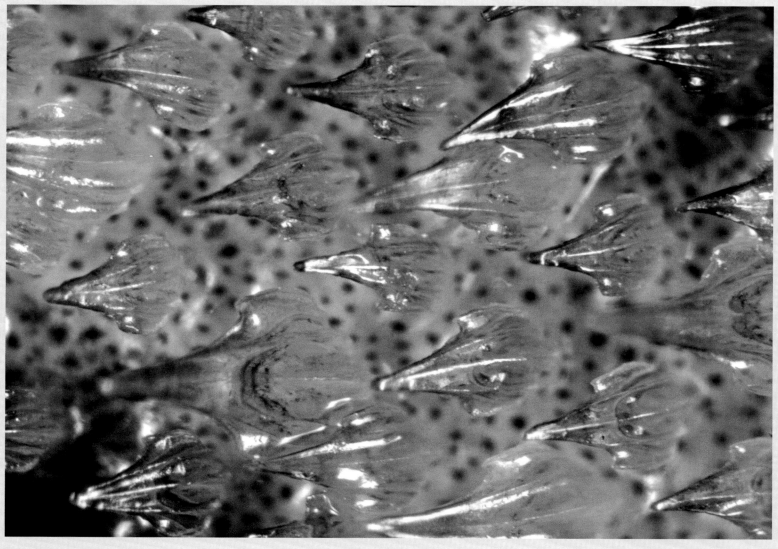

Dogfish (family Squalidae)

Velvet belly lantern shark (*Etmopterus spinax*)

Velvet belly lantern shark (*Etmopterus spinax*)

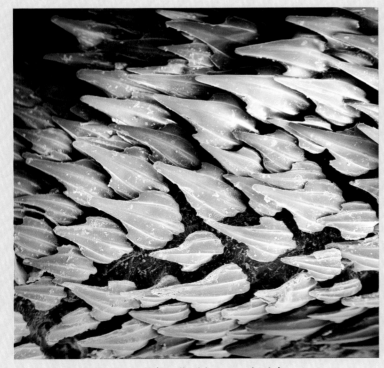

Small-spotted catshark (*Scyliorhinus canicula*)

Small-spotted catshark (*Scyliorhinus canicula*)

Coloration
Reducing Visibility

Sharks are not usually thought of as sporting attractive chromatic attire. The functionality of their coloration is generally more geared toward stealth than to mate attraction. The standard shark color scheme involves countershading, in which the back and upper parts of the body are darker in color while the lower portions of the body and belly are lighter. This effectively camouflages the shark whether it is seen from above — the dark dorsal surface blends with the dark water below the animal — or viewed from below — the light ventrum blends with the sun's rays penetrating from above. For sharks that live above the seafloor, this color pattern works very effectively.

Numerous shark species, however, especially those from coastal rocky or coral reefs, display more intricate patterns that, like countershading, make them less conspicuous in their home habitats. Many of them usually rest on the seafloor, including some of the most attractively marked: the wobbegongs. These sharks can be adorned with spots, bands, lines, saddles or patches of color that help them to disappear against the multihued palette of the reef on which they rest. In some species, such as Ward's wobbegong, the body markings look like "glitter lines" produced by the sun's rays refracted through the water's surface. By blending in with their surroundings, these ambushing wobbegongs gain a predatory advantage.

While the colors of the wobbegongs facilitate prey capture, the epaulette sharks may rely on their color patterns to avoid becoming a meal. As with other reef-dwellers, their many spots and lines help break up their outline and make them less detectable. Many epaulette shark species also sport a dark spot surrounded by a light border on each "shoulder"; these are known as ocelli, or eyespots. When viewed from above, these false eyes appear to be looking back at you, which may dissuade piscivorous predators from attacking the epaulette shark.

Some shark species undergo chromatic metamorphosis as they grow. Many of the bamboo sharks (*Chiloscyllium* species) are boldly marked upon hatching, but as they grow their distinctive bands fade. The markings of their youth, which help break up their shape, may relate to the fact that they are more prone to being eaten when smaller. A similar chromatic metamorphosis occurs in the zebra shark (*Stegostoma varium*). In this species the juveniles are striped (hence the common name "zebra shark") but the stripes break up into spots as the young sharks mature; because of the speckled adult color pattern, this species is referred to as "leopard shark" in some regions.

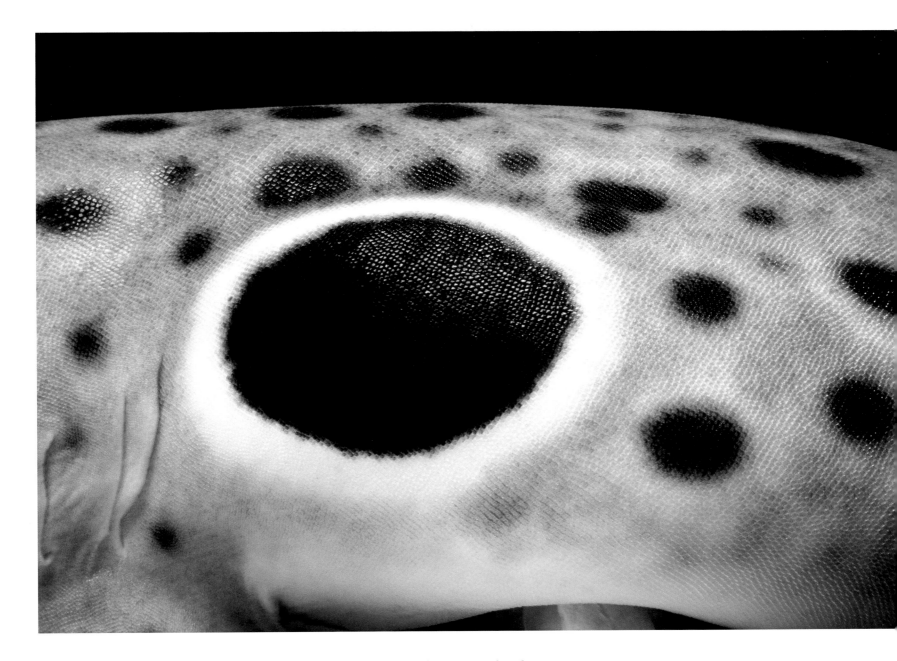

Color patterns may also help sharks recognize members of their own kind. It has been suggested that the black tips on the fins of a number of requiem sharks may facilitate species recognition. These markings differ among the various "blacktip" species and may help a shark locate members of its own kind during social interactions and mating.

Are you being watched? The eyespot (or ocellus) present over each pectoral fin of the epaulette shark (*Hemiscyllium ocellatum*) may look like the head-on view of a larger predator when the shark is viewed from above. This may cause epaulette shark enemies to think twice before attacking the bottom-dwelling shark.

Hasselt's bamboo shark
(*Chiloscyllium hasseltii*)
— juvenile

Hasselt's bamboo shark (*Chiloscyllium hasseltii*) — subadult

Indonesian speckled epaulette shark (*Hemiscyllium freycineti*) — juvenile

Hooded epaulette shark (*Hemiscyllium strahani*)

Horn shark (*Heterodontus francisci*)

Draughtsboard shark (*Cephaloscyllium isabellum*)

Brown-banded bamboo shark (*Chiloscyllium punctatum*)

Northern wobbegong (*Orectolobus wardi*)

Coral catshark (*Atelomycterus marmoratus*)

Zebra shark (*Stegostoma varium*)

Gulf catshark (*Asymbolus vincenti*)

Bioluminescence
Creating Light
in the Deep

Bioluminescence is visible light produced by an organism from a chemical reaction. In vertebrates it occurs only in fish, and more than 50 deepwater shark species (10 percent of all sharks) have light-producing photophores distributed around their bodies. These photophores may play a role in camouflaging the sharks, aid in cooperative behaviors such as schooling or hunting, or help sharks find and select suitable mates.

Only two deep-sea groups are known to glow: two Squaliformes subfamilies, the lantern sharks and the dwarf pelagic sharks. The dwarf sharks are small and hover in mid-water. They likely fluoresce as a counterillumination camouflage, so that from below they are indistinguishable against the dim glow of the surface. A glow-in-the-dark pelvis may provide luminous sexual signals to assist lantern sharks mating in the dark. Lantern sharks generally feed near the bottom and likely use luminescence as a means to aid schooling. Hormones released by the sharks activate their photophores. The velvet belly lantern shark has nine different regions that luminesce; around the pelvis, females glow more brightly than males when hormone levels are seasonally high.

Invisibility cloak. The tiny velvet belly lantern shark (*Etmopterus spinax*) casts an eerie glow. Some 50 thousand photophores are distributed on the underside of the velvet belly. They have a pale blue glow that may render the sharks invisible to predators when viewed from below against the brightness of the sea's surface. (Photos courtesy of Prof. Jérôme Mallefet, research associate, FNRS at UCL)

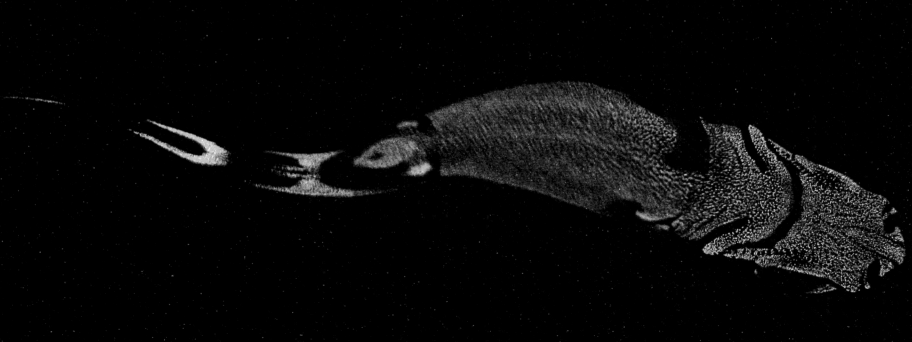

Teeth

The Right Tool
for the Job

Sharks' teeth are primarily a reflection of their diet, so you can guess a lot about a shark's diet simply by looking at its teeth. Some sharks, such as the grey nurse shark (*Carcharias taurus*), have sharp, needlelike teeth that are optimal for grasping and holding small prey such as fish and squid. Other sharks, including the white shark (*Carcharodon carcharias*), have broad, serrated teeth that are perfect for cutting through flesh and removing chunks of tissue from large prey such as marine mammals. Pictured below: Tiger shark (*Galeocerdo cuvieri*) teeth in lower jaw.

What we know best about sharks is their teeth. That is because teeth are the only hard structure in their body, and because they produce so many of them over their lifetime. While their cartilaginous skeletons decompose rapidly, sharks' teeth have remained embedded in layers of sediment, in near-perfect condition, for hundreds of millions of years. The reconstruction of ancient shark taxonomic groups and families is still determined primarily by similarities and differences in tooth shape.

Their teeth are almost as diverse as the sharks themselves, and the shape of each species' teeth reflects its unique predatory specialization. In fact, this specialization can even be seen within a species. Young white sharks eat smaller fish and rays as they are growing and accordingly have pointier, smoother teeth. Only later, as they become adults and begin to shift their diet to seals and sea lions, do they acquire the large triangular serrated teeth they're famous for.

Blue shark (*Prionace glauca*)

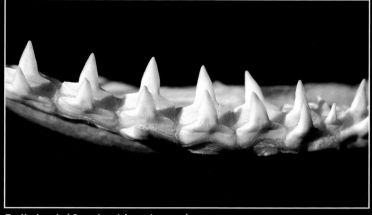

Bull shark (*Carcharhinus leucas*)

Nurse shark
(*Ginglymostoma cirratum*)

Porbeagle shark (*Lamna nasus*)

Grey nurse shark
(*Carcharias taurus*)

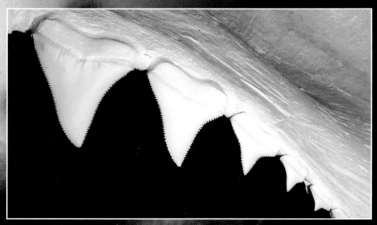

Great white shark (*Carcharodon carcharias*)

Cartilage
Flexible and Light

Cartilage is strong, light and flexible. Teleost fishes, unlike sharks, went on to evolve endochondral skeletal bone, which is formed when bone replaces cartilage during growth and development. However, retaining a cartilage skeleton provided sharks with several key advantages. Cartilage is about half as dense as bone; reduced mass facilitates acceleration, leading to faster bursts of speed when hunting prey. Sharks also do not have swim bladders, as teleost fish do, and the reduced mass allows for greater buoyancy and less effort in swimming. Another key difference is that shark muscles do not attach directly to the bone the way they do in teleosts. In sharks, muscles connect to the dermal layer, a mesh of fiber just below their tough skin. Overall this gives sharks a light, highly flexible and strong body composition, with excellent acceleration strength and flexibility.

The cartilaginous skeleton of a porbeagle shark (*Lamna nasus*), revealed by a CAT scan. The pectoral girdle supports the paired pectoral fins, which form the largest, farthest forward fin pair on the bottom. The pelvic girdle supports the paired pelvic fins, which are the smaller fins behind the pectoral fins. The dorsal fin is above the vertebral column. The fin rays that support the dorsal, pelvic and pectoral fins are called ceratotrichia; they are the part consumed in shark-fin soup. (Photo courtesy of Dr. Steven Campana, Bedford Institute of Oceanography, Canada)

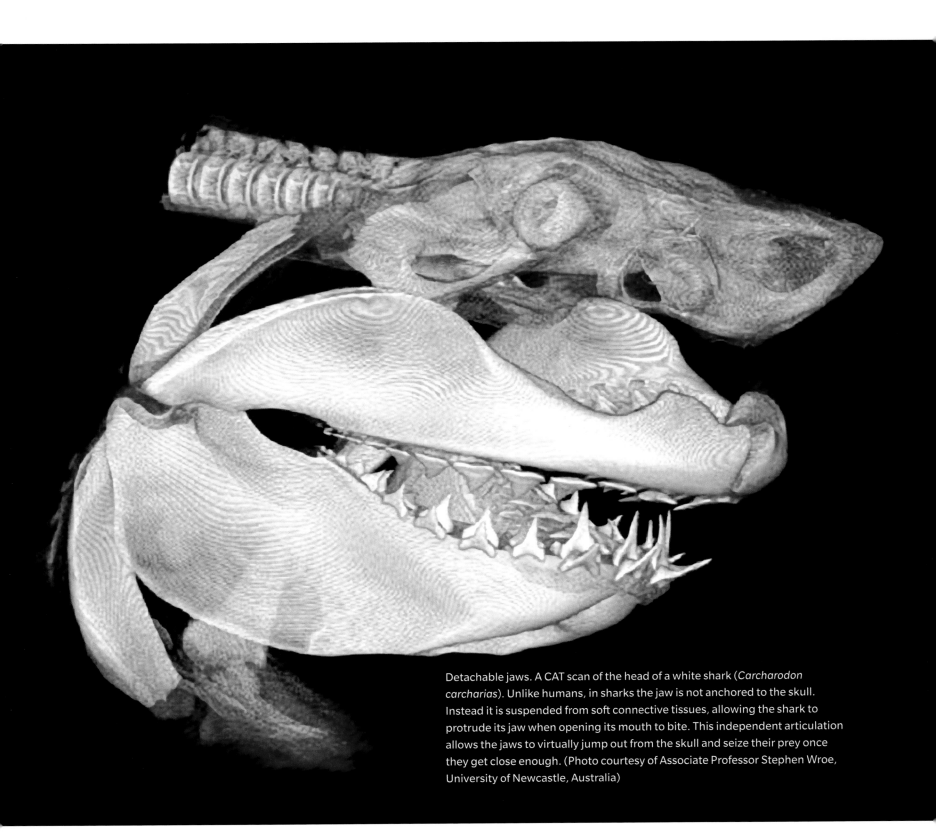

Detachable jaws. A CAT scan of the head of a white shark (*Carcharodon carcharias*). Unlike humans, in sharks the jaw is not anchored to the skull. Instead it is suspended from soft connective tissues, allowing the shark to protrude its jaw when opening its mouth to bite. This independent articulation allows the jaws to virtually jump out from the skull and seize their prey once they get close enough. (Photo courtesy of Associate Professor Stephen Wroe, University of Newcastle, Australia)

Dorsal Fin
More Than What Appears above the Surface

Nothing more distinctively says *Shark!* than the sight of a tall triangular dorsal fin slicing through the water surface. This defining feature has an important functional role in adding stability and maneuverability to the shark's swimming repertoire. Greater fin stiffness is required for stability while flexibility is necessary for tight maneuvers, and sharks are able to accomplish both. Below their skin, sharks' bodies are wrapped in crisscrossing layers of collagen fibers. At the core of a shark's fin are soft cartilaginous radials and highly flexible fin rays, or ceratorichia. The cross-helical architecture of the skin fibers surrounds the entire body in a sheath that extends over the dorsal fin. This sheath is pliable yet capable of rapidly transferring tension. Tension in the skin fibers increases with swimming speed, as the exertion raises internal hydrostatic pressure, essentially "inflating" the shark within its skin. Increasing tension provides greater support for the dorsal fin, similar to the wire rigging supporting the mast of a sailboat. So the faster the shark swims, the stiffer the dorsal fin becomes, providing greater stability at high speeds but regaining flexibility for maneuverability at low speeds.

The dorsal fin of a white shark (*Carcharodon carcharias*) cuts through the water in False Bay, South Africa. The unmistakable triangular shape at once evokes a sense of danger, but the true danger is for the shark — up to 100 million sharks are killed for their fins every year.

OPPOSITE PAGE: Blacktip reef sharks (*Carcharhinus melanopterus*) are so named because of the marking on their fins.

Endothermy
Maintaining a Hot Body

Lamnid sharks have hot bodies. They are endothermic, meaning that unlike the vast majority of fishes they maintain an elevated body temperature, well in excess of their environment. Endothermy is a universal characteristic of all mammals but has evolved independently in some sharks. Only the exclusive Lamnidae family — white, mako, salmon and porbeagle sharks — possesses this ability. Retaining body heat while living underwater is an impressive feat, given that thermal conductivity through water is some 25 times greater than through air.

Endothermy gives lamnid sharks an edge by keeping their muscles and vital organs warm while expanding their niche range to colder and deeper waters. To retain heat, they have special "heat exchangers" in their circulatory system. These radiator-like structures transfer heat from outgoing to incoming blood in their organs and muscles. These heat exchangers, called rete mirabile (Latin for "wonderful net"), are a sponge-like network of thin capillaries where heat can be efficiently rerouted and retained instead of lost to the cold water. Among the lamnids, the most impressive endotherm is the salmon shark, which at times swims in near-freezing water while maintaining a 27°C (80.6°F) body temperature.

High energy. A salmon shark leaps out of the waters of Prince William Sound, Alaska, leaving no doubt as to how this predator earned its name. Salmon sharks aggregate in large numbers each year near the mouths of Alaskan rivers just as the annual salmon spawning runs begin. One study estimated that salmon sharks may consume between 12 and 25 percent of Pacific salmon annually.

A salmon shark (*Lamna ditropis*) swims through the cold, productive waters of Prince William Sound, Alaska. As endotherms (warm-bodied animals), salmon sharks are able to swim faster and outperform the ectothermic (cold-bodied) prey that they hunt, such as Pacific salmon, herring, squid and walleye pollock. This allows them to be highly effective predators in the frigid waters of the North Pacific.

Enlarged Liver
Rechargeable Battery
and Buoyancy Control

Sharks have incredibly large livers filled with rich oil that can account for more than a quarter of their body weight. The liver from a 30-foot basking shark captured off Monterey, California, weighed 816 kilograms (1,800 pounds) and was 60 percent oil. Up to 2,270 liters (600 gallons) of oil has been extracted from the liver of a single basking shark — enough fuel to power a loaded semi from New York to San Francisco. The liver oil is a repository of stored energy that can be tapped when regular feeding is suspended, for example, during migration or mating.

In addition to energy stores, the enlarged liver plays an important role in controlling buoyancy. Unlike teleost fishes, sharks have no air bladder that they can inflate to keep from sinking. The oils in a shark's liver are, by volume, considerably lighter than water, meaning that the liver provides significant additional buoyancy. This buoyancy system has potential advantages over the swim-bladder strategy. The oil does not compress with the increased pressure at depth, so sharks have constant buoyancy at any depth. With an air bladder, on the other hand, teleost fish have to generate more gas, typically oxygen, to counteract its compression as they go deeper, and must expel or reabsorb the gas as they get into shallower waters. Without their liver oil for buoyancy, sharks would exert a tremendous amount of energy swimming upward just to maintain a constant depth in the water.

The dual purpose of the liver sets up an interesting trade-off for sharks that need to swim constantly. When food is plentiful, their livers grow. If feeding is suspended, they are swimming with a fully charged "battery" that they can draw on. However, the more they draw on those reserves, the denser they become. At some point they will have to work harder at swimming in order to maintain their depth.

Despite its being the second-largest shark in the world, much is unknown about the basking shark (*Cetorhinus maximus*). It was long noted that basking sharks disappeared from their normal haunts during the winter, leading some to speculate that they spent the winter hibernating in the deep sea. Satellite tagging has since demonstrated that these sharks do not in fact hibernate on the seafloor but instead are "snowbirds" that move to warm subtropical and tropical waters during the winter. When in the southern latitudes, basking sharks reside in deep water — 200 to 1,000 meters (656 to 3,300 feet) down — which is likely why these sharks were previously never detected at these southern locations.

Sensory Arsenal

Vision

Sharks have well-developed eyes that can function over a wide range of light levels, depending on the particular activities of the species. The bigeye thresher (*Alopias superciliosus*) has the largest eye in relation to body size, but the very largest eye belongs to the white shark (*Carcharodon carcharias*), even though it is relatively small compared with its size. White sharks rely heavily on vision for hunting their prey, and their eyes are suitable for both day and night vision. An eye- and brain-heater called the orbital rete keeps the white shark's eyes warm. This warming system helps buffer the central nervous system from the rapid temperature changes it experiences while diving deep, and warming of the retina improves visual sensitivity and perception.

Smell

When water flows into a shark's nose through the incurrent nostril, it passes through an ellipse-shaped olfactory chamber. The olfactory chamber is filled with wing-shaped epithelium folds known as lamellae. The intricate folding of the lamellae maximizes the surface area that is covered with olfactory sensory cells. The sensory cells are interspersed with tiny beating cilia that increase the water flow over the lamellae, maximizing contact between sensory cells and chemical signals in the water. These fluid-propelling cilia are like tiny fingers flicking and sorting through incoming water molecules, exposing even the tiniest concentration of scent. As a result, sharks have a highly sensitive sense of smell, which they use to find prey, detect predators and even find mates. When they come across a scent trail, they are able to track it back to its source from great distances. Sharks can gain an impressive amount of information from odors. Experimental studies suggest they can smell the difference between a fish that is stressed and one that is not.

Although sharks were long thought to have poor vision, their eyes are highly developed. Like humans, sharks have a dynamic iris that is capable of changing the size of the pupil in response to changes in ambient light. Shark pupils come in all shapes and sizes, ranging from circular to slits with different orientations. Slit pupils, like those of the lemon shark, are typically found in active predators that hunt during the day or night.

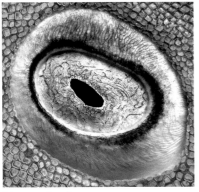

Nurse shark
(*Ginglymostoma cirratum*)

Kitefin shark (*Dalatias licha*)

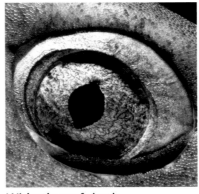

Whitetip reef shark
(*Triaendodon obesus*)

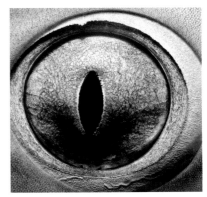

Whitetip reef shark
(*Triaendodon obesus*)

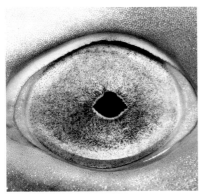

School shark
(*Galeorhinus galeus*)

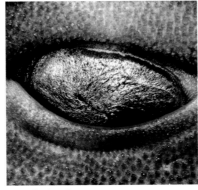

Swell shark
(*Cephaloscyllium ventriosum*)

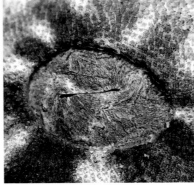

Tasseled wobbegong
(*Eucrossorhinus dasypogon*)

Caribbean reef shark
(*Carcharhinus perezi*)

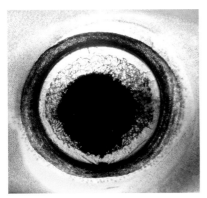

Scalloped hammerhead
(*Sphyrna lewini*)

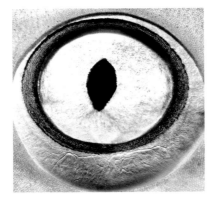

Lemon shark
(*Negaprion brevirostris*)

Port Jackson shark
(*Heterodontus* sp.)

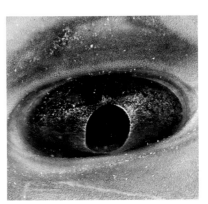

Sawshark
(*Pristiophorus* sp.)

The large eye of the white shark (*Carcharodon carcharias*) contains both cones and rods, allowing the shark to see well in color and in low light conditions, though it appears to be better adapted to daytime vision. Sharks possess a reflective layer of guanine crystals at the back of the retina, called the tapetum lucidum (Latin for "shining carpet"). This layer of crystal plates reflects light back through the retina, providing a second chance for the photoreceptors to detect the light. This greatly increases the sensitivity of shark eyes, allowing them to see well even in dim conditions. During the day, when there is ample light, the tapetum is covered by pigmented cells to prevent overstimulation.

Hearing

Sharks' ears are filled with millions of hair cells, which are composed of a tight patch of cilia grown out to different lengths. Sharks can directionally perceive sounds up to 400 meters (440 yards) away, and their ears are tuned to low-frequency sounds between approximately 40 and 800 hertz (Hz). Free-ranging sharks are attracted to sounds with specific characteristics: irregularly pulsing frequencies below 80 Hz, which are similar to those produced by struggling prey. The inner ear is a labyrinth of tubes and chambers, filled with gelatinous fluid but ultimately open and connected to the outside seawater. Sounds traveling through water as compression waves cause the fluid particles to oscillate within the labyrinth, stimulating the cilia and triggering the perceived signal.

Electrosensing

Any movement of an animal produces an electrical field. Muscle contractions move ions, setting up faint electrical fields that can be detected by a

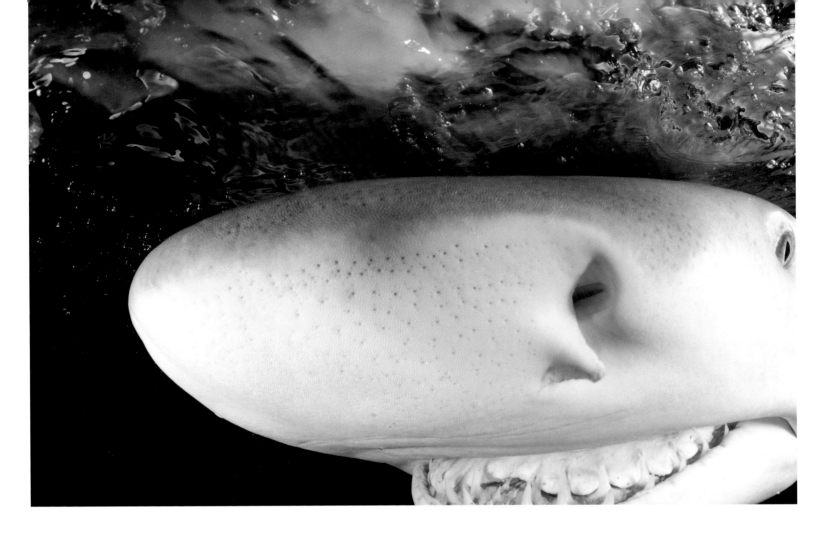

predator at close range. Changes in these tiny electrical fields are not perceptible to animals on dry land, but water is 10 million times more conductive to the flow of electricity than air. Beneath the surface of the ocean even the tiny heartbeat of the smallest fish has a perceptible field, and many ocean predators have evolved the capability to detect such fields in order to locate their prey.

For electroreception, sharks have specialized organs called ampullae of Lorenzini, which appear as small pores around the shark's head and snout. Each pore is an opening to a small canal filled with conductive jelly. Sharks are able to detect the electrical potential across the jelly-filled canal. Hammerhead sharks, with their wider heads, have more ampullae than many other species, which may help explain the broad shape. Electroreception may also explain sharks' incredible ability to accurately navigate long distances at great depths and in total darkness. For navigation, they likely take their cues from Earth's magnetic field or geomagnetic features in the local seafloor, or both.

Sharks can smell in stereo. The large nostrils of the lemon shark (*Negaprion brevirostris*) are set on opposite sides of the rostrum like most sharks. The distance between sharks' nostrils helps them determine which way their food (or mate) lies. If an attractive odor strikes the left nostril first the shark will turn to the left, and vice versa. If their nostrils were very close together as ours are, they would have a hard time determining odor direction. Therefore the wider apart the nostrils are, the more capable a shark is of determining which way to "follow their nose." Hammerhead sharks have the widest distance between nostrils and therefore may have an even greater advantage at locating prey by olfaction.

Calling all sharks. Natives of Papua New Guinea were aware of what sounds sharks can hear well before formal scientific research was conducted. In a practice known as "shark-calling," fishermen use coconut rattles to attract a shark to their canoes, where they carefully capture it by slipping a noose around its neck. The sharks respond to the sound of the rattle because it mimics the noise of a struggling fish. Sharks are highly regarded and important as spiritual animals to the people of Papua New Guinea. Shark-calling is considered a magical practice that requires special training; the process is steeped in ritual, which includes special songs sung to the sharks to entice them into responding to the rattle.

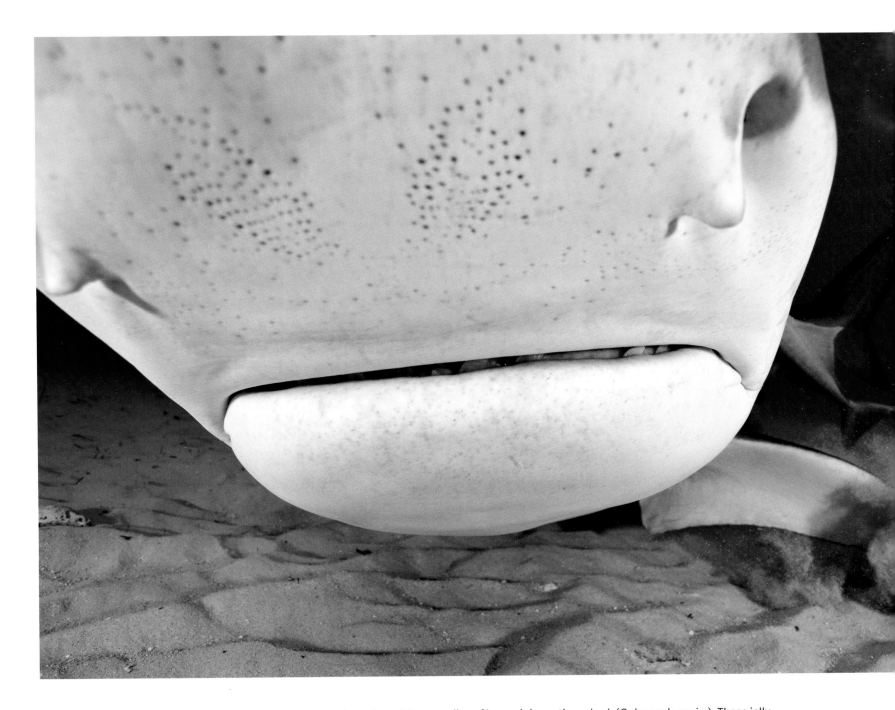

An up-close view of the ampullae of Lorenzini on a tiger shark (*Galeocerdo cuvier*). These jelly-filled "pits" contain extremely sensitive electroreceptors for detecting the electrical fields of prey and electromagnetic fields in the environment for orientation. They are also highly temperature-sensitive, able to detect very small changes in water temperature. This allows sharks to find oceanographic features where prey aggregate, such as a confluence of currents where warmer waters and colder waters come together.

Body Plan

Swimming: Speed Versus Agility

Shark body plans are adapted for a range of swimming patterns, from anguilliform, or eel-like, to the stiffer, high-performance thunniform, or tuna-like, mode. Most shark species fall somewhere in between, in the intermediate carangiform, or mackerel-like, category. Each form has distinct advantages. Anguilliform swimmers are highly maneuverable and capable of very rapid bursts from a stationary position — ideal for ambushing or outmaneuvering prey in close quarters. The undulations ripple through their whole body like a ribbon.

Thunniform swimming is typical of some of the fastest marine vertebrates. Although slower from a start and less maneuverable, they are very stable at high speeds, which they can sustain for long periods to outpace their prey. In thunniforms undulation is confined to a more forward portion of the body. A horizontal keel at the body–tail juncture, called the caudal peduncle, reinforces their stiff tails. It provides hydrodynamic properties that reduce drag, as well as lateral strength for increased thrust. Only the lamnid sharks are considered thunniform swimmers, and they are also endothermic. The extra thrust provided by their thunniform body plan provides additional ventilation (oxygen) to the gills, supporting the high metabolic demands of endothermy.

Dynamic Lift: Flying Underwater

To keep from sinking, sharks need to "fly" through the water. But in place of wings, sharks have enlarged pectoral fins. The surface area and foil action of their pectoral fins generate lift as they move forward in the water — the same mechanism for the lift force generated by an airplane or bird wing. Some shark species, such as nurse sharks and wobbegongs, can rest on the bottom and move water through their gills by pumping their buccal (cheek) cavities. But active species have lost this ability and need to swim forward with their mouths open in order to continually ventilate their gills. For these obligate ram-ventilators, lift is critically important. Without adequate surface area to generate lift, the effort required to counteract their negative buoyancy and maintain their depth would be overwhelming.

Shark swimming modes range from the eel-like (anguilliform) to a stiff-bodied tuna-like (thunniform) style, though most sharks fall in between those extremes. The sevengill shark (*Notorynchus cepedianus*), left, is very flexible and its sinuous undulations extend through the length of its body. At the other extreme, the body of the white shark (*Carcharodon carcharias*), right, remains relatively stiff throughout. Instead of a tapering tail, the white shark has a wide keel at the base of its tail — the caudal peduncle — which helps to maintain that stiffness and delivers a powerful stroke.

The oceanic whitetip shark (*Carcharhinus longimanus*) is named for its large, winglike pectoral fins (*longimanus* is Latin for "long hand"), which provide the shark with lift and allow it to efficiently move great distances in the open ocean. The oceanic whitetip spreads its majestic wings globally; it is one of the most wide-ranging of all shark species, occurring in tropical and subtropical seas around the world. It was also once suggested that it might be the most abundant animal, weighing more than 45 kilograms (100 pounds) on the face of the Earth. Killed for the very prized fins that have enabled them to glide throughout the world's oceans, oceanic whitetips are now scarce over much of their range. In fact, their species is considered critically endangered in the northwestern and central Atlantic Ocean and is only occasionally seen where it was once common in other regions of the world.

Even though the oceanic whitetips were once ubiquitous, there is still much to learn about their secret life. Research suggests the young are born in the open ocean, not in coastal nursery areas as with most other requiem sharks. The conspicuous white markings on the tips of their fins may play an important role in the foraging behavior in the open ocean. From a distance, all that can be seen of oceanic whitetips are the bright white tips of their fins. These markings may resemble a small school of fish, attracting tuna, dolphinfish or other prey species into striking range of the shark. While adult sharks have the bold white fin markings, young sharks bear black blotches in place of their elders' brilliant livery. Because smaller oceanic whitetips are vulnerable to predators, it is important that they be less conspicuous to open-ocean enemies, and so they begin life with muted fin blotches for concealment that, as they grow, transform into the white fin lures of the adult.

The blue shark (*Prionace glauca*), with its impressive "wingspan," is one of the most widely distributed species of shark. Whereas the oceanic whitetip is circumglobal in tropical water, the blue shark ranges around the globe in slightly cooler subtropical to temperate waters. Blue sharks are capable of deep dives but generally occupy the upper 200 meters (650 feet) of the water column. They prefer temperatures ranging from 10 to 20°C (50 to 70°F) and as they apporach the warmest most equatorial reaches of their range they exhibit a phenomenon known as "tropical submergence," in which they shift to deeper cool water to avoid the warm surface they normally inhabit. As a pelagic (open ocean) shark, the blue shark is constantly on the move and, not surprisingly, travels enormous distances. These sharks are known to cross ocean basins; one blue shark was recaptured 9,200 kilometers (5,700 miles) from where it was tagged. Blue sharks are all about efficiency. Their broad pectoral reach provides for energy savings through dynamic lift and gliding. When they undertake long migrations such as across the Atlantic Ocean, they can also exploit oceanographic features, utilizing major ocean currents to help them along.

Tail: Thrust Generator

Sharks' tails generate twice the number of water jets as those of other fishes. Sharks are able to form a "dual-ring vortex" by activating specific muscles during the middle of the stroke. This stiffens the tail as it straightens out, generating thrust throughout the tail-beat rather than just at the beginning and end of the stroke. This unique quality is likely to be an adaptation to help maintain more constant lift, necessary for overcoming sharks' negative buoyancy, and ultimately may make for more efficient swimming.

The tail of a white shark (*Carcharodon carcharias*) is more homocercal ("same tail" in Greek) than that of most sharks: the upper and lower lobes are nearly the same length. Homocercal tails are extremely efficient at high speeds and produce little drag, making them effective for extensive cruising. They are typically found in highly active open-ocean sharks that move great distances, such as the mako shark (*Isurus oxyrinchus*) and salmon shark (*Lamna ditropis*) in addition to the white shark.

The tail of the sevengill shark (*Notorynchus cepedianus*) is strongly heterocercal, which in Greek means "different tail" and refers to the longer top lobe of the caudal fin. As this shark beats its tail from side to side, the upper lobe generates lift because it is at an angle to the animal's horizontal body plan, as well as thrust to propel the shark forward. The lift produced by the tail is counterbalanced by the flat anterior surfaces of the shark's head and its pectoral fin. Heterocercal tails are effective at generating bursts of speed, allowing sharks to accelerate rapidly and maneuver in the pursuit of prey.

4

Strategies & Behaviors

Sharks have been typecast by Hollywood as dangerous wandering rogues of the sea — solitary, opportunistic, indiscriminate killers. But while sharks may travel alone at times, they are far from being vagrant drifters. Many sharks travel vast distances along pre-established migratory routes according to precise seasonal schedules to get from feeding grounds to mating grounds to birthing areas. They are capable of precise navigation through mechanisms that remain a mystery to this day. Some aggregate in vast schools with complex social structures and hierarchies. They can show restraint, allowing small fish to approach and remove parasites. Sharks also exhibit a broad spectrum of highly specialized feeding strategies, taking advantage of the different food resources available in the ocean, but some are generalists, able to feed on a large range of different prey types. The more we study sharks, the more complex and fascinating behaviors we discover.

A lemon shark (*Negaprion brevirostris*) opens wide for a cleaning. Knowing when to bite and when to allow bite-sized fish to swim in and out of its mouth benefits both shark and cleaner. Lemon sharks have long been observed gliding down to rest on the bottom for the sake of oral hygiene. Studies have shown that they will even suspend breathing (pumping their gills) for more than two minutes while the cleaners are at work. This must take some concentration, as the shark needs to almost triple its respiration rate to "catch its breath" once the cleaner fish has exited.

Homing Instincts

Returning to the Motherland

Just as salmon return to their native stream to spawn, many sharks also return to their birthplace to have pups. It remains a mystery how sharks are able to remember and find their birth site. For instance, though they roam wide and far, great white sharks tend to bear their pups in the same area where their ancestors birthed for hundreds of thousands of years. Female white sharks from South Africa are known to traverse the ocean to Australia, but their site fidelity is so strong that they will always return to their native Africa to pup. Similarly, female white sharks off California regularly venture thousands of miles from the coast but have returned for generations to pup in the same region.

A result of natal homing is that maternal lineages become genetically isolated. California white sharks are genetically different from those across the ocean off Japan and from those off New Zealand. Despite white sharks' capacity for ocean crossing, they have returned faithfully to their respective homelands since the Late Pleistocene — some 200,000 years.

A white shark (*Carcharodon carcharias*) swims just underneath the surface off South Africa. White sharks are known to undertake large migrations, moving enormous distances and then returning to the same location, in a behavior known as site fidelity. In a display of incredible navigation and endurance, one shark tagged in South Africa swam across the Indian Ocean to Australia and then returned to where it was tagged in South Africa, traveling a distance of more than 20,000 kilometers (12,500 miles) in less than nine months.

Long-Distance Migration

Salmon sharks travel south after gorging on salmon in Prince William Sound, Alaska. They swim as far as Mexico, only to return to the mouth of the same river the following year in time for another salmon run. White sharks regularly migrate thousands of kilometers across the open ocean, from the coast of North America straight to Hawaii, and find their way back precisely to their favorite seal rookery. The journey takes more than a month each way. Their ability to find a tiny island in the vast open ocean is a feat of navigation that modern humans can accomplish only with the aid of maps and navigational tools. Sharks must have a mental map and some directional cues to accomplish the same. However, what cues sharks use remains a mystery; possible mechanisms include celestial navigation and geomagnetic sense.

A white shark (*Carcharodon carcharias*) flanked by tiny pilot fish (*Naucrates doctor*). Pilot fish do not in fact pilot sharks on their long migration; rather, they follow. But to keep pace with such large and powerful swimmers, they ride an invisible pressure wave created near the front of the shark as its forward movement parts the water; this makes it appear as though the shark is following them. Pilot fish will actually defend their shark from others of their own species, actively flashing their colors while chasing them away.

Yoyo Diving

Many open-ocean sharks engage in a behavior known as yoyo diving that has puzzled scientists for some time. Yoyo diving, as the name suggests, is a general term that refers to repeated up and down movements through the water column. This same, or similar, diving pattern may be a result of very different shark behaviors including prey location, regulation of internal temperature, and energy conserving travel.

One hypothesis is that the up and down diving pattern may paradoxically be the most efficient means to swim a distance from one location to another. In theory a shark may conserve energy if, instead of swimming constantly in a straight line, it exerts energy in bursts — climbing up in the water column, then gliding slowly down while maximizing the distance along its course. This pattern of "undulating flight" is a form of energy-conserving locomotion that was first noted among birds. However, given sharks' ability to achieve lift using enlarged pectoral fins, it is not surprising that at least two species, the great white and whale shark, have been recently found to exhibit undulating flight in water. Researchers made this discovery by attaching accelerometer data loggers (similar to the motion-detecting devices found in most smart phones) to the dorsal fins of whale sharks, or by feeding the instruments to great white sharks. The data recorded on these tags was then used to determine when a shark was beating its tail versus passively gliding in relation to their ascents and descents (shown in the accompanying figure). In these examples the intermittent locomotion bursts and rests in the upper half of each graph clearly correspond with the climbing and diving respectively, confirming the undulating flight behavior. Whether this ultimately translates to an energy savings or not remains to be determined; nonetheless undulating flight is one likely explanation for yoyo diving in sharks.

Data loggers attached to a great white and whale shark reveal for the first time that both sharks perform an "undulating flight" swimming pattern consisting of a cyclical rhythm of climbing and then gliding. The black line charts the sharks depth over time while the red line deviates up and down with each swaying tail beat, and rests near zero when the shark is still. Among birds, this is known to be an energy saving mode of locomotion, more efficient than straight line flight. (Reproduced with permission; Gleiss et al. 2011)

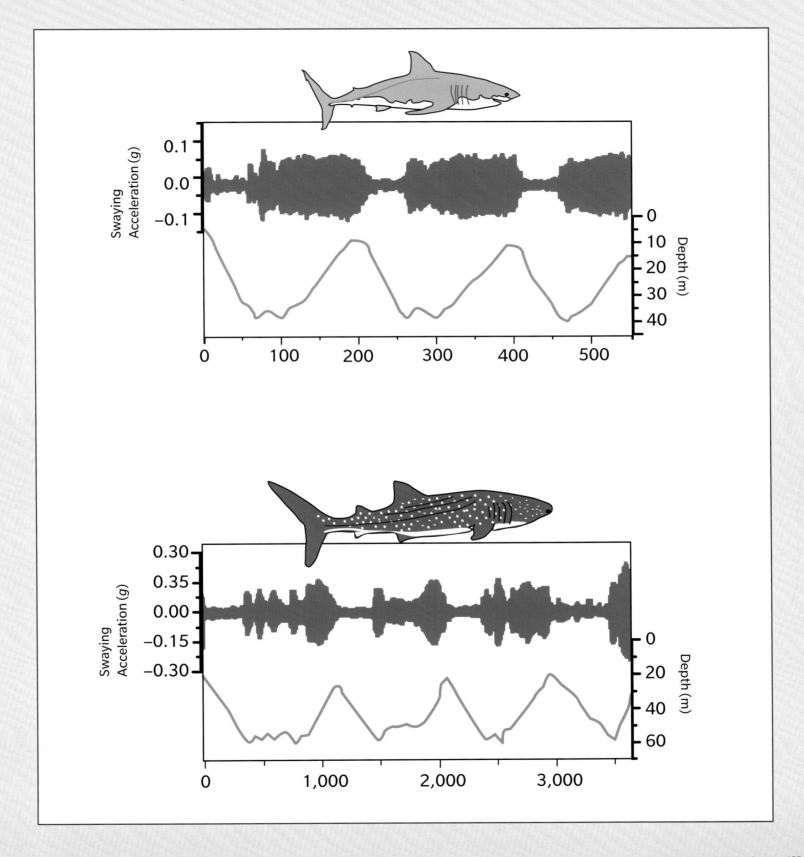

An alternative explanation for yoyo diving has to do with locating smells. By diving through the various water layers, a shark may locate and follow chemical scent trails that could lead to food concentrations or potential mates. Chemicals do not move as freely up and down in the water column because of the increasing density of colder water layers; in essence each warmer layer floats above the next and resists mixing. Thus a shark moving from one temperature layer to the next can expose its sensory equipment to new chemical cues and potentially new food sources. For example, basking sharks are thought to respond to dimethyl sulfide, a substance released by phytoplankton as it is being consumed by the zooplankton that these sharks target. Swimming vertically across thermal layers increases the chances of intersecting a scent plume that is diffusing horizontally within a layer. On the other hand, when prey are located deep in colder water, sharks may need to limit their exposure, having to thermally recover near the warm surface before venturing down again to forage at colder depths. The necessity for thermal regulation by some species, particularly the endothermic (warm-bodied) species such as makos, great whites and salmon sharks, can result in the same yoyo pattern.

Many sharks are visual predators that gain an advantage when approaching prey from below — more easily tracking their target silhouetted against the bright sea surface. This is the primary hypothesis for how white sharks locate and capture pinniped prey near the surface. However, this same mechanism may also be at play in deeper water for a variety of shark species. Blue whales are known to track dense patches of krill from below when they are similarly backlit, lunging through the thickest clouds. It therefore seems possible that yoyo diving in species such as the whale shark could also result from repeated runs at zooplankton patches from below.

A pair of whale sharks (*Rhincodon typus*) make steep descents. Repeated yoyo diving by whale sharks could be explained by a variety of behaviors. Their planktonic prey often occur in thin layers along a particular depth, so moving up and down through different layers may be the fastest way to locate them. Furthermore, their meal may be easier to spot silhouetted from below than when viewed horizontally. And when on the move to a distant location, they may employ an energy-saving "climb and glide" mode of locomotion.

Lean, Mean and Clean

Visiting Cleaning Stations

A number of bony reef fishes acquire nutrients by picking off parasites, necrotic tissue and mucus from the bodies and fins of other fishes. More often than not the species that are cleaned are other bony fishes, but some elasmobranchs also enjoy these cleaning services. Of the more than 140 bony fish species known to clean other fishes, 12 are known to take on their cartilaginous neighbors as clients. This includes species in the angelfish, butterflyfish, stripey, wrasse, goby and remora families. Some elasmobranch cleaners, such as the cleaner wrasses (*Labroides* species), depend solely on parasite-picking for nourishment — they are known as obligate cleaners. Others, including the king angelfish (*Holacanthus passer*), consume parasites only on occasion; species that clean part-time are known as facultative cleaners.

Cleaner fishes typically enjoy immunity from becoming a snack of a potential client. However, there are always exceptions to the rule. Wobbegongs will occasionally inhale a cleaner wrasse, while the sand tiger shark has been reported to ingest sharksuckers (*Echeneis naucrates*). Remoras have also been found in the stomach of whale sharks, although the ingestion incidents were probably accidental. Parasites consumed by shark cleaners include isopods, copepods and flatworms. These pests, which feed on the body tissues and fluids of their hosts, can be found on head, body and fin surfaces, on the gills, around the cloaca and in the mouths of sharks.

Two types of cleaning strategies have been recognized in bony fishes. The first is employed by the remoras (see page 174 for more on these), which attach to a shark and inspect and clean their cartilaginous companion. The other strategy involves parasite-picking fishes that "set up shop" at certain locations on the reef known as cleaning stations. Scientists studying shark-cleaning episodes off the coast of Brazil suggest that some reef-dwelling sharks are more likely to visit reef-associated cleaners when remoras are rare in the area. Cleaning stations are often on conspicuous reef pinnacles or in caves or crevices. Seamounts also serve as important grooming stations for sharks. In order to reduce their parasite load, open-ocean species such as the pelagic thresher shark will visit seamounts specifically to enlist the services of cleaner wrasses. The threshers visit so regularly that dive operators can almost

guarantee "elasmophiles" an opportunity to see this otherwise rarely encountered shark.

When a shark visits a cleaning station and wants to be groomed, it will often adopt a specific posture to communicate its desire. This position also enables the cleaner to better inspect it for ectoparasites. Sharks will expand their gill slits, distend their jaws and reduce their swimming rate to help the parasite-feeding fish accomplish their work. The pelagic thresher shark engages in a behavior called circular-stance swimming, in which the shark slows its pace, raises it head and swims in a circle. Likewise, scalloped hammerheads will reduce their swimming rate when being inspected and cleaned by adult king angelfish; they may move so slowly that they begin to sink. (Both the thresher and hammerhead sharks are obligate ram-ventilators — in order to respire effectively, they must push water over their gills by swimming forward.) In contrast, when being inspected by tiny yellownose gobies (*Elacatinus randalli*), the Caribbean reef shark, a species that can effectively remain still, pumping water over its gills, will rest peacefully on its side or belly during cleaning bouts.

Pelagic thresher sharks (*Alopias pelagicus*) roam the open ocean in search of small fish to eat. However, they come to seamounts (underwater mountain peaks) not to eat but to feed the smaller fish. Local seamount fishes are more than happy to accept the delivery — external parasites that have latched on to sharks. Thresher sharks swim slowly over fixed "cleaning stations" where small wrasses and other reef fish have gathered in anticipation. As a shark makes a hovering pass over the cleaning station, the little cleaners briefly leave the protection of the reef, darting up to pluck off the copepods and other parasites, particularly on the fins and pelvic areas of the thresher sharks.

A scalloped hammerhead shark (*Sphyrna lewini*) glides slowly over a cleaning station where the butterflyfishes known as barberfish (*Johnrandallia nigrirostris*) are gathered. They eagerly pluck crustacean parasites from the shark's underside. These small fish know they can safely swim right up to the mouth of the shark. This understanding is likely signaled by the body language of the shark — a distinctive "pose" that lets the fish know it is safe to approach.

Some of the most ubiquitous parasite-pickers on Indo-Pacific reefs are the cleaner wrasses (genus *Labroides*). A blue-streak cleaner wrasse, *Labroides dimidiatus*, is seen here inspecting the head of a grey reef shark. These crayon-sized cleaners may inspect and groom as many as 2,000 client fish in the space of a day. While cleaning of sharks by bony fishes has not been well studied to date, preliminary research indicates that parasite-pickers can play an important role in the daily activity and local distribution of certain shark species.

A king angel fish (*Holacanthus passer*) reaches in to snack on a parasite behind this scalloped hammerhead's rostrum. The king angelfish lives on shallow reefs and seamounts in the Eastern Pacific, where hammerheads typically aggregate.

Along for the Ride

Remoras, or diskfishes may look like parasites, but they are parasite predators, providing some benefit to their shark host by relieving them of parasitic copepods. Rather than waiting for a shark or ray to visit a specific cleaning area, these fishes hitch a ride, inspecting and picking parasites from their elasmobranch host at their convenience. The remoras are highly specialized, possessing a suction-cup-like dorsal fin they use to attach themselves to the body surface of their host. As juveniles they tend to reside in the mouth, gill chambers, anus and spiracles of the shark, either for protection or possibly to avoid competition with larger members of their own kind. In the case of larger shark species such as the whale shark, it is not unusual to see large numbers of these fish attached to the same shark.

The remora family consists of eight species, with three species that regularly associate with sharks and rays. Their dependency on their shark partners varies among the species. Some feed heavily on the crustacean ectoparasites, while the bulk of the diet of other species consists mainly of zooplankton and small fishes they capture along the way. Additionally, they scavenge scraps of food during shark feeding events and even consume the placentas of viviparous sharks during pupping.

The shark is more than a swimming buffet for the remora; it also provides a means of transportation and protection. By associating with large, toothy sharks, remoras reduce the likelihood of being eaten themselves. The relationship is considered mutualistic — both shark and remora benefit from the association. However, in some cases these hitchhikers leave abrasions on the shark's skin and appear to annoy their host. Sharks have been seen jumping out of the water or rubbing against the seafloor in an apparent attempt to rid themselves of their hangers-on.

TOP: Remoras, or suckerfishes, often occur in large numbers on their host, in this case a lemon shark (*Negaprion brevirostris*). Their modified dorsal fin enables them to adhere using suction. The spines in the fin are split into movable ridges, known as laminae, inside a fleshy disc. The remora presses the disc against its host and moves the ridges like the slats in a window blind. This creates a powerful suction — the suction force of the disc of a large remora can be as great as 45.5 kilograms (100 pounds). When the fish wants to release its grip, it simply folds down the ridges.

BOTTOM: The modified dorsal fin of the sharksucker (*Echeneis naucrates*) looks like a footprint on the top their head. This remora is a coral-reef dweller that spends its time free swimming or attached by its "sucker" to a diversity of hosts including sharks. Studies have shown that young individuals "prefer" to associate with parrotfishes and trunkfishes, but as they grow larger, they tend to hitch rides on reef sharks. Juveniles are partial to copepod parasites, but these crustaceans do not form a significant part of the adult diet. The sharksucker is classified as a coral-reef species that has a "loose" commensal relationship with a variety of hosts.

In the open ocean, remoras are much more dependent on their host since separating, even briefly, could leave them unprotected and vulnerable to other predators. Consequently, these mutualistic partnerships are likely to be long-term with high fidelity to the host on which they first settle. Remoras move freely around their host's body. The safest attachment on this oceanic whitetip shark (*Carcharhinus longimanus*) may be just below its mouth like a goatee; what predator would dare pursue this remora? In addition to grooming their host, remoras will snap up tiny fishes and zooplankton along the way, and when the shark is feeding, they may also enjoy the occasional crumb that "falls from the master's table."

Social Interactions

A school of scalloped hammerhead sharks (*Sphyrna lewini*) moves together at Cocos Island, Costa Rica. Researchers have noted that during these daily gatherings the sharks show no interest in feeding. The hammerheads maintain a roughly equal distance from each other, in all directions, as they circle around underwater landmarks such as seamounts or islands. At nightfall they move off alone or in smaller groups to feed in the surrounding deep water.

Scalloped hammerhead sharks (*Sphyrna lewini*) form massive schools around seamounts and oceanic islands. Every night they move off, singly or in small groups, to feed in the surrounding deep water, and every morning they return. During the day they do not feed but circle together in swarms over the seamount, staying close together, swimming slowly as if in a trance. For hammerheads, these daily gatherings are thought to be beneficial for conserving energy, transmitting information and facilitating social interactions such as mating. Schools of hammerhead sharks observed at seamounts in the Gulf of California are often composed primarily of females, the largest of which compete for a prominent position near the center of the school. This hierarchical structure may be a way to signal their fitness and status to male suitors.

Safety in Numbers

For smaller sharks — juveniles that are not yet apex predators — schooling together provides safety in numbers. A single young shark would expend more energy and be less effective at staying alert for potential danger. Sharks within a large group can rest, swimming slowly in a familiar area, and be more assured that approaching danger will be detected early. Juvenile lemon sharks actively associate with other individuals of a similar size. As a result, schools of juvenile sharks tend to be of a similar age. Many juvenile sharks, including hammerheads, bonnetheads and blacktip, lemon and bull sharks, spend their early years schooling in shallow coastal nursery areas. The schooling behavior is thought to be mainly for predator avoidance; however, it may also help the fish hunt more efficiently.

A group of juvenile lemon sharks (*Negaprion brevirostris*) moves through mangrove roots in the Bahamas. Nursery habitats are often in shallow, protected areas such as mangroves, where larger predators don't occur and there is ample food. However, protection from predators often trumps food availability in the case of certain nursery areas. During their first year of life, as many as 93 percent of juvenile scalloped hammerhead sharks (*Sphyrna lewini*) starve because of lack of food in their nursery area, Kane'ohe Bay in Hawaii. There are few large predators in Kane'ohe Bay, so even when food is scarce, the protection afforded by this shallow, murky bay makes it a better place to hide than other, riskier spots more open to the deep ocean.

Seamount Aggregations

For sharks that ply the waters of the open ocean, a seamount rising abruptly from the seafloor provides a landmark in an otherwise vast undifferentiated expanse. Seamounts may have multiple benefits for the sharks that aggregate there. In addition to being a place where they can come to get parasites cleaned off, to interact and possibly to mate with other sharks, seamounts provide a well-defined marker from which the sharks can stage their movements to known foraging areas at night. Every night, scalloped hammerhead sharks are able to wander 20 kilometers (12.4 miles) from a central seamount to feed; they return by morning, often along the same pathway. Their keen sense of orientation is likely aided by their ability to detect magnetic stimuli. Magnetic particles in the seafloor have distinctive patterns of distortion around volcanic seamounts. The result is a magnetic-anomaly "landscape" of ridges and valleys that we can visualize only with the aid of a sensitive instrument called a magnetometer. Sharks, however, are believed to be capable of detecting minute magnetic field distortions by using their ampullae of Lorenzini. Since a hammerhead shark's ampullae are spread out over the broader area of its rostrum, this may give it more of a "three-dimensional" magnetic sense.

The scalloped hammerhead shark (*Sphyrna lewini*) is believed to use its highly sensitive electroreceptors, the ampullae of Lorenzini, to sense changes in Earth's magnetic field. By detecting these invisible cues, hammerhead sharks are able to navigate through the apparently featureless open ocean. The large surface area of the cephalofoil (the "hammer" part of the head) provides ample room for electroreceptors, giving the scalloped hammerhead the greatest number of electroreceptors of any shark.

Foraging Strategies

Sharks have long been portrayed as indiscriminate, insatiable eating machines. Stories of shark bellies holding odd items — soft drink bottles, aluminum soup bowls, a carpenter's square, cigar boxes, a flashlight, a bongo drum, a bottle of wine, a reindeer — abound in popular literature. However, these anecdotes most likely represent the absurd and memorable exceptions and have come to reinforce a longstanding fearful narrative. In truth there is a vast diversity of ocean animal prey that sustain sharks (not including manufactured objects) and sharks as a group display a dazzling array of morphologies and strategies to successfully exploit these prey throughout myriad ocean ecosystems.

Some shark species exhibit great dietary breadth, eating a wide range of food types, while others are highly specialized eaters. For example, the bonnethead shark feeds mostly on crabs, the crested Port Jackson shark targets sea urchins and the zebra shark specializes in eating shelled mollusks. Dietary specialists often exhibit distinctive morphology that reflects their particular predatory trade. For example, members of the smoothhound shark family have teeth that are well suited for clutching and crushing the carapaces of the crabs on which they specialize, while the needlelike teeth of the sand tiger shark are adapted to grasping small, slippery fishes. The shape of the jaws and how they are suspended from the skull also determine a shark's ability to specialize. Some species, such as the bullhead sharks, have heavy jaws that are tightly buttressed against the skull, with large muscles that enable them to crack open heavy-shelled invertebrates. The specialist strategy generally allows a predator to take advantage of more obscure and less exploited resources, thereby freeing itself from competition with other predators.

The blue shark (*Prionace glauca*) feeds most heavily on relatively smaller prey items, showing some specialization for small schooling bony fishes and squid. Unlike many other members of the requiem shark family, the blue has long gill rakers that prevent small fishes and invertebrates from escaping through its gill slits. While smaller fishes and squid may be a blue shark staple, their broad serrated teeth allow them to also target larger fare, such as whale and dolphin carion, seabirds and other sharks.

In contrast, generalist foragers are able to take advantage of a whole range of prey species. For instance, blue sharks in some seasons and locations forage almost exclusively on schools of small baitfish, while at other times they focus on squid. But if they come upon a drifting whale or dolphin carcass, they are equally capable of portioning off large bites of blubber. Generalist foragers have the advantage of being opportunistic, so that if a single prey item becomes more difficult to acquire, they are versatile enough to exploit other quarry as they become available. The trade-off to this bet-hedging strategy is that generalist species may not be ideally adapted to target any one particular prey item.

Both specialist and generalist strategies have been extremely successful for sharks, enabling them to expand their dietary reach throughout the oceans; however, the breadth of sharks' diet does not extend to plants. There are no known sharks that are herbivorous ocean grazers. The large planktivorous sharks, such as the whale and basking shark, consume zooplankton (animals) and not phytoplankton (plants). While plants are not part of the diet per se, some sharks incidentally ingest plant material and at least one species may intentionally consume large quantities of seagrass. The bonnethead shark is thought to eat seagrass not for its nutritional value but to protect its stomach from the sharp spines on the carapace of its favorite prey, the blue crab.

Two additional contrasting strategies further define shark foraging adaptations. There are those shark species that actively pursue their prey, relying on speed and endurance — for instance, lamnids such as the mako, or carcharhinids such as the blue or lemon shark. In contrast to these more streamlined active sharks, there are slew of sedentary shark species, which rest on the bottom, conserving energy while waiting for prey to come to them. These bottom-dwelling species, such as angel sharks and wobbegongs, tend to be cryptic, often with coloration or shapes that help them blend into their surroundings, ensuring that they remain undetected by their prey.

From invertebrates to whales, the lemon shark (*Negaprion brevirostris*) is a generalist forager that feeds on a range of prey items. It has a short upper jaw that is loosely suspended from the skull. This can be protruded to nimbly pluck a small crab off the ocean floor or to penetrate and scoop a hunk of flesh from the flank of a bloated whale carcass.

Sedentary species such as the banded wobbegong (*Orectolobus halei*) do not eat very frequently, but they also do not exert much energy while waiting patiently for their prey to draw nearer. These carpetsharks position themselves strategically on the reef where small fish tend to school. Consequently, they are frequently seen shrouded in clouds of small fishes, like these bullseyes (*Pempheris* spp.), which are snapped up one at a time when they stray too close.

Filter Feeding

The largest sharks exploit Earth's greatest source of protein: the tiny animals adrift throughout the oceans that are known collectively as zooplankton. To feed their huge bodies, filter-feeding sharks must sift through massive amounts of water, removing minute prey with specialized gills that act as sieves in addition to providing oxygen. Every day a single whale shark filters more water — 2,445,000 liters (645,900 gallons) — than an entire metropolis the size of Miami might drink in the same period. The two largest shark species, the whale shark and the basking shark, resemble whales in their size and feeding niche. A third giant, the megamouth shark, is a denizen of the deep that is also a filter feeder.

It is no coincidence that so many of the ocean's plankton-grazers are giants. Larger individuals can engulf disproportionately more water than can smaller specimens, providing more food per unit effort than could be predicted from their size alone. This allometric scaling implies that selection may occur toward a larger optimal size for filter feeders. Additional advantages may be that large size reduces predation risk and allows retention of metabolic body heat, improving functioning in cold water.

The cavernous mouth of the second-largest shark in the world, the basking shark (*Cetorhinus maximus*), is capable of filtering enormous volumes of water. The white structures in the throat are gill arches that support the shark's gills, which are used to breathe. The gill arches of a basking shark also support structures called gill rakers, which extend across the gaps between the arches and act as a sieve, straining food out of the water. Once enough prey has been filtered from the water, the basking shark will close its mouth and swallow the prey. During the winter many basking sharks shed their gill rakers, which would suggest that they stop feeding. Why they do this remains a mystery, but it may be related to the recently discovered migrations they make to warm southern waters.

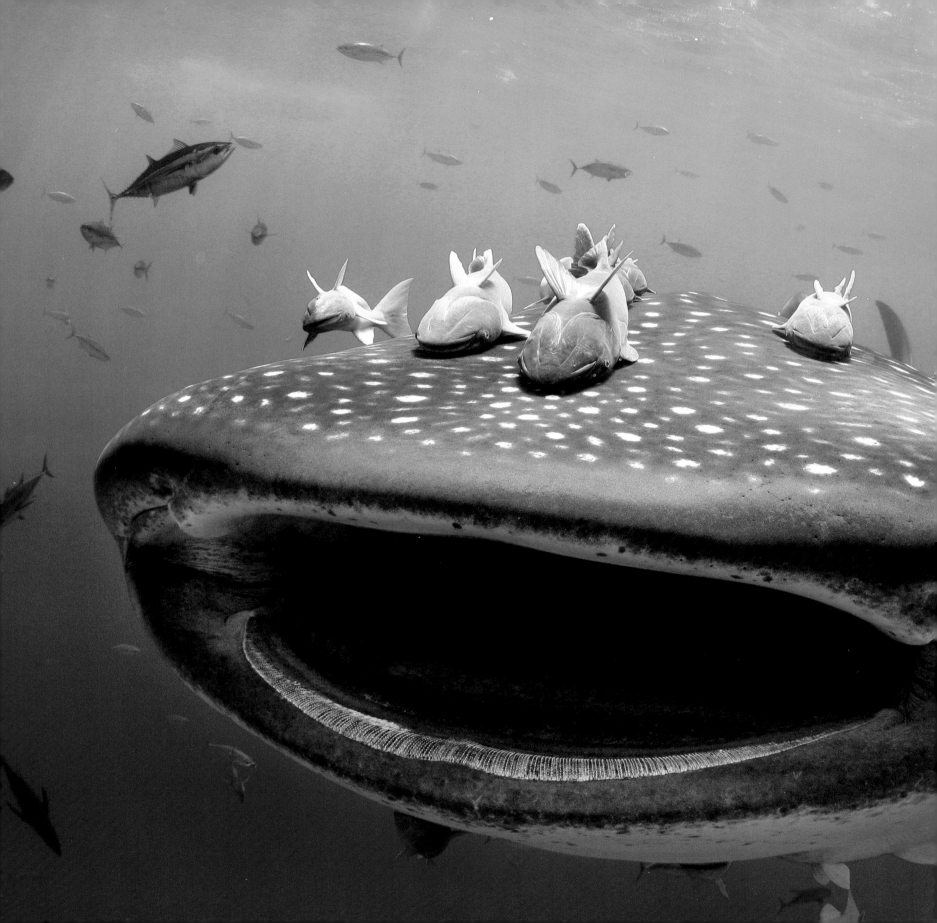

The whale shark (*Rhincodon typus*) is the largest shark in the world, exceeding lengths of 12 meters (40 feet). Both basking and whale sharks use the passive filter-feeding method of swimming slowly with mouth open known as ram-jet ventilation. However, the whale shark has some additional filter-feeding strategies. With its strong throat and gill pouch musculature, a whale shark can actively draw prey in using suction generated by rapidly gaping its mouth. This technique is often used while oriented vertically in the water, often at the surface, with the head amid an aggregation of prey. Whale sharks also "skim" the water surface when tiny prey are concentrated in the top film. This is accomplished by swimming along with their mouth open and partially out of the water, reducing resistance and filtering only the water with the highest prey concentration. Whale shark aggregations are often associated with fish or coral spawning events, where they strain through clouds of eggs. These spawning events occur at particular seasons and lunar phases, and whale sharks have a keen sense of when and where these regular events happen. Despite long wandering migrations, they often reappear at a familiar spawning site with precise timing.

Scavenging

The telltale crescent shape of a white shark's bite on a floating whale carcass. The serrated triangular teeth of these sharks are ideally shaped for stripping the blubber from whale carcasses. Whale blubber is very high in calories and an important food source for white sharks. As endotherms (warm-bodied creatures) living in cooler waters, they have high metabolic demands.

Wherever there is a floating whale carcass in the ocean, you can be certain that sharks will not be far behind. Whale blubber is highly sought after by numerous shark species because of its high caloric content. There is no evidence that even the largest sharks will pursue live whales, but once whales die from other causes, sharks are ready to scavenge. As a whale carcass decomposes, a film of oil radiates out into the surrounding water. Because oil floats on water, it forms a film over the surface that spreads very widely, dispersing quickly and attracting sharks from a large radius. Finding a whale carcass is a windfall for white sharks, and they will stay with the carcass, feeding until they are completely sated. Whale blubber is concentrated in a layer just below the skin; the sharks carefully bite off the blubber layer as if they were eating corn from the cob.

The blubber of a whale represents a treasure trove of energy for a hungry white shark (*Carcharodon carcharias*). It has been estimated that 30 kilograms (66 pounds) of whale blubber can sustain a 4.6-meter (15-foot) white shark for more than a month and a half. Often numerous white sharks will converge on a dead whale; a social hierarchy forms in which only one shark feeds at a time — the largest shark feeds first and progressively smaller sharks feed afterward.

Parasitism

RIGHT: The mouth, jaws and tongue of the cookie-cutter shark (*Isistius brasiliensis*) have evolved for quickly and efficiently removing plugs of tissue from larger animals. When it bites, the shark latches on to the larger animal by plunging its lower teeth into the victim's flesh while using its upper lip to create suction. It then twists its body, removing a plug of tissue from the undoubtedly surprised larger animal and creating a characteristic craterlike wound. To a cookie-cutter shark, anything larger than itself represents a potential meal — it is ready to sample everything it comes across. These sharks have been known to attack such unpalatable items as underwater cables, hydrophones deployed from naval ships, and even nuclear submarines.

OPPOSITE PAGE: Many species fall prey to the cookie-cutter shark, including tuna, marlin, dolphinfish, seals, dolphins, whales and even the megamouth shark (*Megachasma pelagios*). Bites ranging from fresh wounds to healed-over scars are frequently seen on many marine species, attesting to the frequency of cookie-cutter attacks in the open ocean. A long-distance swimmer attempting to cross the channel between Hawaii and Maui recently had the misfortune of being the first human to be attacked by one of these sharks. After unsuccessfully biting the man on the chest, the persistent little cookie-cutter tried again; in the second attempt it managed to remove a characteristic plug of tissue from the man's calf.

Sharks' large investment in highly specialized and replaceable teeth is one of the keys to their success in exploiting a wide range of resources. Ironically, the largest teeth relative to body size belong to a small parasitic shark that has been dubbed a "mosquito of the sea." The razor-sharp triangular teeth of the cookie-cutter shark (*Isistius brasiliensis*) and the largetooth cookie-cutter shark (*I. plutodus*) are ideally suited for excising a circular piece of flesh from unsuspecting hosts, in much the same way that a melon baller works. While these diminutive dogfish — they are only 50 centimeters (20 inches) long — can consume whole small prey such as squid, they are best known for rising from great depths at night to target much larger quarry, including swordfish, tunas, larger sharks and even whales.

Unlike most other sharks, which shed and replace single teeth at a time, cookie-cutter sharks shed entire rows at once, probably to ensure that there are no gaps, which could impede a clean, quick bite. As the rows of teeth are shed, much like a set of dentures, they are swallowed, a practice that may help the sharks reclaim some of the large amount of calcium invested. Cookie-cutter sharks also have bioluminescent photophores on their undersides that emit the strongest light of any known shark. Viewed from below, the green light they emit closely matches the glow from the surface, a camouflage technique known as counterillumination.

Ambushing

Some sharks acquire their food by doing less. Instead of actively searching for prey, they simply remain motionless and wait for unwary prey to come too close. This hunting tactic, known as ambushing or sit-and-wait hunting, is not possible for obligate ram ventilators, which must swim constantly to ventilate their gills. Consequently, only the buccal pumpers, that can respire while waiting cryptically, hunt this way. Angel sharks, wobbegongs and certain catsharks are known ambushers.

Angel sharks enhance their concealment by partially burying themselves under the sand. When a cephalopod or small fish moves within an inch or two of its head — *wham!* — the shark erupts from the sand and slurps up the unsuspecting victim. The swell shark uses a different technique. It will rest on the bottom and suck up blacksmith damselfishes that get too close to its head — known as gulp hunting — or simply open its mouth and let the oblivious damsels drift right into its gaping jaws; this latter technique is known as "the yawn."

Another catshark, the pyjama catshark (*Poroderma africanum*), typically lives on rocky reefs and spends the daylight hours hiding in caves and crevices. It does most of its hunting at night, feeding on octopuses, squid, crustaceans and bony fishes as they slumber. However, when squid spawn in communal egg beds, these sharks will take up ambush sites among the piles of squid eggs resting on the seafloor. Although the squid will swim off if they spot a shark moving into the egg beds, they gradually habituate to its presence and will return to deposit their eggs near the stealthy predator. When a female descends to deposit her eggs near the shark's head, the cunning predator pounces on the careless cephalopod.

The Australian angel shark (*Squatina australis*) is a cryptic hunter. When an unsuspecting fish, crustacean or cephalopod gets too close to its head, it will lunge into the water column and throw open its jaws, at the same time rapidly expanding its gill and mouth cavities. Now you see it, now you don't! — its quarry suddenly disappears into the shark's maw. Angel sharks that live near rocky reefs will usually select an ambush site near the reef–sand interface because of the greater density of potential prey around the rocks.

For their size, the swell sharks (genus *Cephaloscyllium*) have some of the widest jaws of any shark species. They use their expansive maw and numerous, sharp grasping teeth to good effect, capturing an assortment of invertebrate and fish prey. The diets of two swell shark species have been extensively studied and include burrowing worms, snails, squid, octopuses, hermit crabs, spiny lobster, stalked tunicates, other sharks, elasmobranch egg cases and an extraordinary assortment of bony fish species (from slippery conger eels to armored boxfishes). The Japanese swell shark (*Cephaloscyllium umbratile*) even eats electric rays! The head of a slumbering swell shark (*C. ventriosum*) is shown here.

Luring

Some ambushing sharks take their stealthy craft up a notch. These species employ anatomical adaptations to lure potential prey into the strike zone. In some cases this luring takes on a passive form. For example, the wobbegongs sport colors that help them blend with the reef substrate, and skin flaps around their head look like encrusting invertebrates and/or plant material. A bony fish or crustacean that mistakes the motionless wobbegong for food-rich substrate or even as a potential hiding place is likely to get a big surprise.

The active oceanic whitetip shark may rely on a more passive form of luring to attract other active fishes. In the blue pelagic environment, the counter-shaded oceanic whitetip would be almost invisible from a distance if it were not for the bright white blotches on most of its fins. When they see them from afar, tuna and other piscivorous bony fishes may mistake these conspicuous markings for a group of smaller fish; this is known as the "spot-lure" theory. If a tuna made a run at this pseudo-school, it might find itself within sprinting range of the vigilant whitetip before it could divert its attack.

It is possible that some deep-sea sharks also lure prey with their light-producing organs. The cookie-cutter shark bites chunks from marine animals larger than itself, scooping out mouthfuls of flesh with its unique dentition.

The cookie-cutter may lure targets within striking range with the help of light-producing photophores. This shark has numerous small photophores on its belly that are thought to obliterate the outline of the shark when it is viewed against the light coming down from the ocean's surface. The black collar around its "neck" lacks photophores; when viewed from below, it has the shape of a small fish. A predator looking upward may cue in on that shape and attack. Of course, the attacker then becomes the attacked and ends up losing a plug of flesh to the parasitic cookie-cutter.

The most amazing shark lure is the tail of the tasseled wobbegong (*Eucrossorhinus dasypogon*). This shark, considered the most specialized member of the wobbegong clan, is unique in that when it is in repose, its tail is always curled up. The tasseled wobbegong turns out to have special talents that involve its coiled caudal fin. When it sees a potential prey item, the shark will raise its tail and wag it back and forth like a friendly puppy's. When it does this, the lower lobe of the caudal fin resembles a small swimming fish, complete with eyes. Neighboring reef fishes may mistake this pseudo-fish for a potential food item or possibly a territorial invader. But if they try to attack it, they end up inside the maw of the cunning wobbegong.

The tasseled wobbegong (*Eucrossorhinus dasypogon*) is a master puppeteer — swishing its tail back and forth to resemble a small fish, complete with eyespot. The audience, and potential next meal, is mesmerized and approaches for a close look, maybe its last.

Rather than wait for its quarry to amble past, the tasseled wobbegong (*Eucrossorhinus dasypogon*) uses its curled-up tail to tempt fish prey into striking range. Tasseled wobbegongs are the only species in the family with a curly tail. The inset photo shows the fish-like caudal fin of a luring wobbegong, complete with the false eyespot and apparent tail.

Crevice Hunting and Grubbing

Coral and rocky reefs are replete with cracks and crevices in which invertebrates and fish can shelter. Likewise, soft substrate can provide a blanket that conceals the presence of prey species from hunting sharks. Some sharks are equipped anatomically and/or exhibit specialized behaviors that enable them to utilize these prey resources. Some sharks that live on rocky or coral reefs have very elongated bodies and heads and are almost eel-like in their movements. Epaulette, bamboo and reef-dwelling catsharks can wiggle into rocky crevices or between coral branches to gain access to hidden prey.

The whitetip reef shark is a larger species that is also a master crevice hunter. After dark the diurnally quiescent whitetip begins actively moving over the reef, plunging its head into cracks and crevices in search of sleeping fishes and octopuses. Hungry whitetips will twist and turn violently in their attempts to penetrate deeper into a crevice; some sharks may squirm into a hole on one side of a patch reef only to exit through an opening on the other side. Whitetips will also chase and capture nocturnal fishes that feed over the reef at night, such as squirrelfishes, and snap at fish that have been stirred from slumber by their frenetic activity.

There are also sharks that excavate prey from sand or mud. For example, the Port Jackson shark will place its mouth over the burrow of a clam or worm and suck water and sediment into its mouth, expelling it through the gills. It will do this until it succeeds in displacing enough substrate that the prey item is exposed. Leopard sharks will also use suction — produced by rapidly expanding the size of the mouth and gill chamber — to slurp echiuroid worms from their U-shaped burrows in the mud.

TOP: While often quiescent during the day, whitetip reef sharks come alive at night. They prowl over the reef looking for slumbering fishes or octopuses tucked away in crevices. Groups of whitetips will swarm portions of the reef, diving into reef interstices in an attempt to extract hidden prey.

BOTTOM: The nurse shark (*Ginglymostoma cirratum*) is the bulldozer of the shark clan, using brute force to get at concealed prey. It will displace coral colonies or chunks of coral rubble by shoving its snout underneath these structures, then turn them over by lifting its head. It will also employ suction power to slurp hiding prey from holes in the reef.

Herding Baitfish

Two bronze whalers (*Carcharhinus brachyurus*), mouths full of sardines, plunge through a bait ball of sardines during the sardine run off KwaZulu-Natal, South Africa. The occurrence of bronze whalers off this coast appears to be tightly linked with the annual sardine run. They, and many other shark species, are seen in large numbers as they move in to feed on this seasonal resource.

Numerous shark species target an important ocean resource: giant schools of energy-rich "baitfish" such as sardines. Off South Africa the annual spawning run of sardines (*Sardinops sagax*) presents an opportunity to stock up for predators such as the dusky shark. Large dusky sharks have been captured with masses of sardines in their stomachs, weighing more than 10 percent of their body weight. Sardines and other similar schooling fish are rich in oils. Since sharks store energy in the form of oils in their liver rather than as fat, growing dusky sharks take full advantage of the available feast. Following the annual arrival of the sardines, dusky sharks' livers become enlarged as they amass important energy reserves. To capture their prey, the sharks circle the schools and then rush in, slashing through the swirling masses of baitfish, when a patch becomes dense enough.

Grey reef sharks (*Carcharhinus amblyrhynchos*) and tuna feed on a bait ball of fish in the Solomon Islands, South Pacific Ocean. At times different species of predators seem to work side by side to feed on large schools of baitfish such as sardines. Sharks, tunas, dolphins and other predators will work simultaneously, corralling the fish into a compact, swirling ball trapped against the surface. Once the bait ball is compressed and sufficiently dense, the predators begin rushing through it at high speeds, gulping mouthfuls of fish as they go. Seabirds also join in on the action, diving into the bait ball from above. This spectacular event generally ends only once the entire school of fish

An aerial view of sharks herding a school of baitfish into a ball off the coast of Palm Beach, Florida. Several shark species were identified feeding on this same bait ball, including tiger sharks (*Galeocerdo cuvier*), great hammerhead sharks (*Sphyrna mokarran*), bull sharks (*Carcharhinus leucas*), spinner sharks (*Carcharhinus brevipinna*) and blacktip reef sharks (*Carcharhinus melanopterus*).

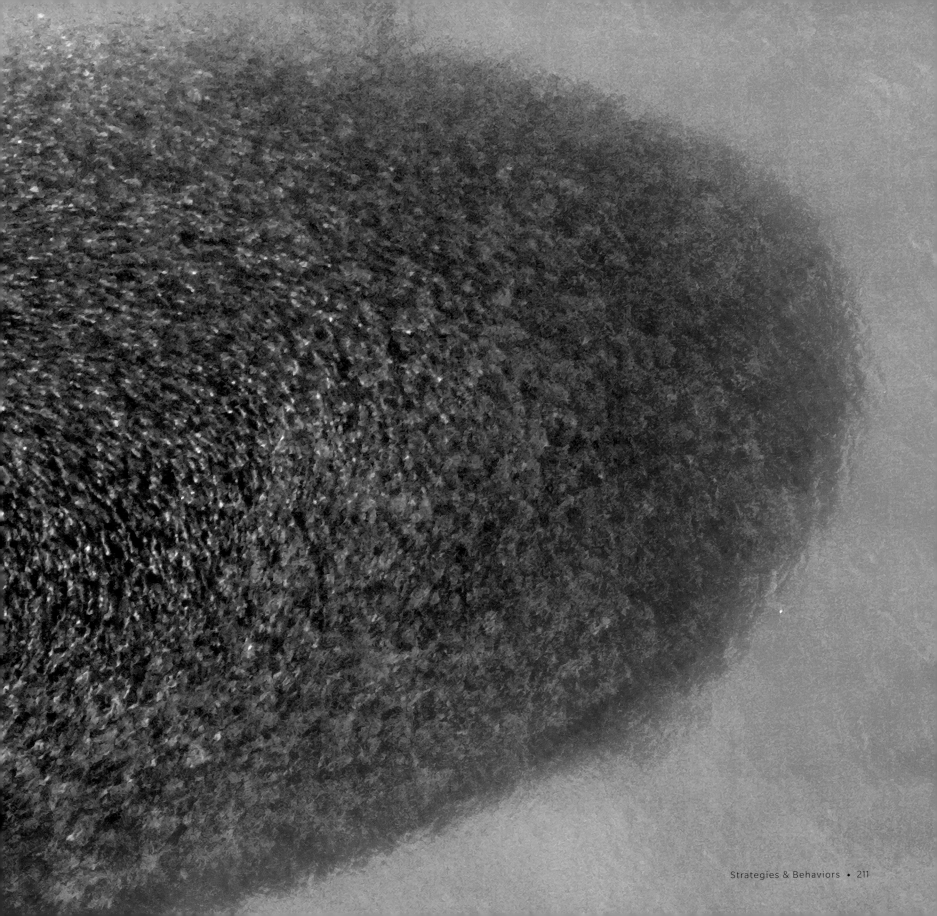

Reptiles on the Menu

When we think of potential shark prey, most of us don't think of reptiles. But oceangoing reptilians make up a significant part of the diet of least one species: the tiger shark. Other than humans, tiger sharks (*Galeocerdo cuvier*) are the primary turtle predators. Aided by their large cutting teeth, wide mouth, powerful jaws and considerable size, adult tiger sharks frequently feed on sea turtles in certain locations such as Australia and the Philippines. They will eat both hatchlings — one individual had 10 young loggerhead turtles in its stomach — and adult turtles, which they may swallow whole or bite into smaller pieces. The range of the tiger shark overlaps that of many sea turtle species; they are known to prey on green, loggerhead, hawksbill and olive ridley turtles.

Tiger sharks will take advantage of turtles' breeding and egg-laying assemblages. For example, at Raine Island on the northern Great Barrier Reef, more than 5,000 turtles converge in a single night to go ashore to lay their eggs. Solitary or in groups, tigers gather around the island, on the reef flat and at its edges, for several months during the sea turtle breeding season. They attack turtles as they make their way to the shore and feed on turtles that die of exhaustion and are washed back into the sea with the falling tide. Anecdotal accounts even tell

In some cases shark attacks on turtles are not lethal. It is not unusual in areas where tiger sharks are common to find turtles with missing flippers, bite marks on the carapace or even chunks of the shell and body removed by a shark bite. In Shark Bay, Western Australia, loggerhead turtles (*Caretta caretta*) are more often seen with shark-inflicted wounds than green turtles (*Chelonia mydas*). Among the former, as many as 50 percent of the males and 25 percent of the females had been mauled but not killed outright by sharks. Scientists suggest that the difference in these wounds is a function of the green turtle's being faster, more maneuverable and stronger than the loggerhead, and thus more likely to evade tiger shark attacks. The hawksbill turtle (*Eretmochelys imbricata*) in this photo has lost a flipper to shark attack.

of tiger sharks nearly beaching themselves as they attempt to capture turtles making their way into the shallows and onto the beach.

Sea snakes also make their way into shark bellies, with the tiger shark being the most frequent serpent eater. Apparently the highly toxic venom of the sea snake does not dissuade a hungry tiger shark. In Australia, for example, sea snakes are frequently found in tiger shark stomachs. These sharks exhibit a dietary shift when it comes to their reptile-eating proclivities. Off New Caledonia, smaller tiger sharks feed more on sea snakes, while larger adults eat a greater number of turtles; off Queensland, Australia, sea snakes are important prey for all tiger shark size classes, while sea turtles are eaten only by adults.

The tiger shark (*Galeocerdo cuvier*) is the primary reptile-eater among shark species, although there are other sharks that eat turtles on occasion. These include the bull shark (*Carcharhinus leucas*), which feeds on smaller coastal sea turtles, and the white shark (*Carcharodon carcharias*), which feeds infrequently on turtles but is a known predator of the leatherback sea turtle (*Dermochelys coriacea*).

Mammals as Prey

A white shark investigates a seal decoy from below. Their inquisitive nature has led these sharks to bite an array of strange objects, including crab pots, buoys, boats, kayaks, float and bags; their teeth have even been found embedded in logs. Because sharks don't have hands, they use their mouths to inspect things. Many white shark attacks on humans seem to have been investigatory rather than predatory in nature; unfortunately, even a very gentle investigatory bite from a white shark is capable of causing grave injury. Humans appear to be unpalatable to white sharks, probably because they lack the blubber that the sharks seek. In most cases the victim is released after the investigatory bite, which is why most people survive their encounters.

Marine mammal blubber may be the most concentrated, energy-rich food source in the ocean, but few sharks are equipped to acquire it. Mammals' fat is stored under their skin as a layer of blubber. It acts like a blanket, insulating their warm bodies from the heat-sapping water, and also serves as an energy reservoir. This concentration of calories would be highly desirable for any predator, but marine mammals are not easy prey. Whales are big. Dolphins are fast. Seals and sea lions are more attainable, but even they are agile and able to escape onto land.

The consummate master of seal hunting is the great white shark (*Carcharodon carcharias*), and patience may be its strongest suit. White sharks often spend days or even weeks patrolling around a seal colony without securing a meal. Swimming slowly and patiently, minimizing their use of stored energy,

they wait for their chance. When the opportunity presents itself, they can explode in a burst of energy, often propelling their massive bodies clear out of the water.

The seasonal arrival and coastal phase of white sharks in central California is timed to coincide with the presence of young-of-the-year elephant seals, who are naive and plump. When the shark finally gets its chance, it can consume an entire elephant seal, weighing 100 to 150 kilograms (200 to 300 pounds), in only three or four bites. Its laser-sharp serrated teeth and massive jaws enable the shark to cut up and consume the seal quickly, before the shark's opportunistic peers arrive. A single such meal can last a white shark a month and a half or more. Other sharks that target marine mammals include large makos (*Isurus oxyrincus*), tiger sharks (*Galeocerdo cuvier*) and Greenland sharks.

White sharks (*Carcharodon carcharias*) are stealthy hunters that swim along the bottom looking upward for prey. While the dark coloration on their backs blends in with the bottom, making it difficult for prey to see them from above, white sharks can easily see prey silhouetted against the brightly lit surface. Once a potential prey item has been identified, white sharks will launch spectacular attacks, rushing vertically at high speed and often launching out of the water.

Not all white shark attacks are successful; a steep learning curve is associated with feeding on highly maneuverable and alert prey such as seals. One study indicated that only about half of their attacks were successful. In addition, it appears that age brings wisdom to white sharks. They become more effective hunters as, through trial and error, they develop more successful hunting techniques. With experience, white sharks also learn where the most productive hunting spots are, and will return to specific locations year after year.

Shark Predators

Many shark species, including the broadnose sevengill, bramble, prickly, great white, sand tiger, bignose, bull and great hammerhead sharks are opportunistic shark predators. Most of these not only prey on other shark species but will also engage in intraspecific predation, where they consume their own, typically smaller, congeners. Female sharks often fast when visiting nursery grounds to give birth, a likely adaption resulting in reduced infanticide. Aside from other sharks, however, sharks have few natural predators.

Probably sharks' next most important predators are the toothed whales (odontocetes). Of this group, the killer whale (*Orcinus orca*) most often hunts sharks and rays. When feeding on sharks, these whales may consume the entire animal or selectively ingest the more nutrient-rich body parts (particularly the oil-rich liver), leaving the remains for scavengers. Some killer whale pods are actually shark specialists and consume a variety of species, including sleeper, whale, basking, thresher, mako and hammerhead sharks. Killer whales that specialize on sharks show pronounced tooth wear; their teeth are ground flat by the abrasive sharkskin denticles. Killer whales have even been witnessed capturing and consuming the liver of a great white shark. Some sharks, such as the broadnose sevengill, have been known to beach themselves in a desperate attempt to escape from marauding killer whales. By contrast, the only shark that regularly feeds on killer whales is the parasitic cookie-cutter shark; in certain regions these cetaceans regularly bear the telltale wounds and scars of *Isistius* attacks.

Sperm whales are also known shark predators, although they feed primarily on squid. In New Zealand waters sperm whales occasionally eat bramble and kitefin sharks. In Canada's St. Lawrence River estuary these whales feed on Greenland sharks, while off the coast of Sulawesi, Indonesia, a pod of sperm whales was seen attacking an enormous megamouth shark.

Some large bony fishes also consume sharks. The grouper family contains several behemoths that are known to ingest young or smaller chondrichthyan species; these include the goliath grouper (*Epinephelus itajara*) and the giant grouper (*E. lanceolatus*). While not an important predator of elasmobranchs, saltwater crocodiles eat the occasional shark that shares its estuarine habitats.

OPPOSITE PAGE: The killer whale (*Orcinus orca*) is one of the few natural shark predators. There are a number of different killer whale ecotypes defined largely by diet specialization. Some killer whales forage almost exclusively on marine mammals, while others are piscivorous, eating only fish. In the northeastern Pacific ocean killer whales of the "offshore" ecotype are frequently observed hunting and consuming Pacific sleeper sharks (*Somniosus pacificus*). Off the coast of New Zealand, certain pods are considered elasmobranch specialists, with 80 percent of their diet comprising elasmobranchs of at least 10 different species.

While seals and sea lions often fall prey to larger sharks, on occasion these marine mammals will turn the tables and prey upon smaller shark species. For example, fur seals have been seen capturing and feeding on angel sharks, wobbegongs and catsharks.

There are two fishes that parasitize sharks. Lampreys, jawless fish resembling a large leech, have been reported to latch on to a handful of shark species, but they only cause minor damage. The pugnose eel (*Simenchelys parasitica*) is a more insidious parasite. These alien-like eels burrow into the shark's musculature and then work their way into the body cavity, where they feed on internal organs such as the heart. "Death by eel" is apparently not a common occurrence, but it has been reported in the smalltooth sand tiger and the shortfin mako shark.

Sharks are afflicted by a number of different ectoparasites that feed on the tissue and body fluids of the host. Crustaceans — copepods and isopods — are some of the most common shark ectoparasites. They may attach to the eyes of the Greenland shark, resulting in blindness in many of their hosts, or line the rear edge of the dorsal fin of shortfin mako sharks so that the long tails of the parasite look like trailing white streamers, as seen here. Sharks also host an array of internal parasites, namely monogenetic flukes, tapeworms and nematodes. Being a host to these parasites does not come without costs; they can cause anemia, reduced respiratory efficiency, skin disease, slowed development of the reproductive organs, slowed growth and death.

5

Threats & Hopes

After reigning supreme for more than 400 million years, suddenly, in a virtual blink of the eye, sharks are no longer the ocean's top predators. Today that role has been usurped by humans — and our effect on sharks is massive. On average fewer than 6 human deaths per year are caused by shark attacks. In contrast, up to 100 million sharks are killed annually by humans, 70 million of which are used to make soup from their fins. Why do we kill so many sharks, and what are the consequences? Is 100 million a lot? (By comparison, according to the US Department of Agriculture, 8 *billion* chickens are slaughtered each year in the United States alone).

Ironically, the very qualities produced by sharks' unique evolutionary lineage have also made them a prized target for consumption. In today's market, sharks are highly sought for the cartilage in their fins, which are used to make shark-fin soup that sells for as much as US$100 per bowl. Sharks are also hunted for the oil in their massive livers, for their specialized skin and their teeth, and simply as trophies. Similarly, the unique qualities of their life history, their late maturity and their high investment in few and large offspring make shark populations particularly vulnerable to fishing.

As markets have evolved over the years, the demands for shark products have come in surges. Interest in shark-liver oil, for example, dates back hundreds of years. In the 18th and 19th centuries it was used in oil lamps for lighting. Just prior to and during the Second World War (1939–45) there was a strong demand for liver oil for the production of vitamin A. Today shark fins have become one of the world's most lucrative fishery commodities. There is also a high demand for shark cartilage for numerous (unproven) medical benefits. With the current world population of humans exceeding 7 billion, what does the future hold for one of Earth's most ancient and majestic predators?

Shark fisheries have historically experienced boom-and-bust cycles in which landings of sharks are initially high but decrease steadily until the fishery collapses. This pattern is due to the life-history characteristics of sharks, which make them very vulnerable to overexploitation. Because sharks generally take a long time to mature and have few young, they simply cannot reproduce fast enough to sustain industrial-scale fishing unless the fishery is rigorously monitored and quotas are enforced. However, such regulations have historically been difficult to negotiate. (Photo courtesy of Julie Anderson, www.sharkangels.org)

Seen here is a school of scalloped hammerheads (*Sphyrna lewini*) at Cocos Island, Costa Rica. The fact that hammerhead sharks gather in large numbers at predictable locations makes them particularly vulnerable to capture. Hammerhead sharks' fins are considered to be among the most valuable types. Their flesh, however, has low value, given its poor quality for eating. Chances are high that once captured, their bodies will be discarded at sea and only their fins retained.

Fortunately, scalloped hammerheads have recently received protection under CITES (the Convention on International Trade in Endangered Species of Wild Fauna and Flora) along with the great hammerhead (*Sphyrna mokarran*), smooth hammerhead (*Sphyrna zygaena*), oceanic whitetip (*Carcharhinus longimanus*) and porbeagle shark (*Lamna nasus*). However, once the fins are removed, it is difficult for authorities to distinguish whether they came from protected or unprotected species.

Shark Products on the Market

Shark-Liver Oil

Although shark-liver oil has been in use for hundreds of years, it was really Hitler and a perceived vitamin deficiency that fueled the first "gold rush" on sharks, in the early 1940s. Before the Second World War the global source of vitamin A was Scandinavian cod-liver oil. In the months leading up to the Nazi occupation of Scandinavia, the region's fishing and shipping were interrupted, resulting in a worldwide shortage of the vitamin. However, pharmacists noted that large quantities of vitamin A could be extracted from the high-quality squalene oil in sharks' large livers.

The sudden shortage led to a spike in the price of shark-liver oil. Buyers began searching for new sources in regions farther from the fighting, and fishermen raced to cash in on this new interest. In 1947 Otto Isler of Hoffmann–La Roche introduced a commercial synthesis of vitamin A, which paved the way for industrial production of the vitamin and eventually made liver extraction obsolete. World production of shark-liver oil has since declined by a hundredfold; however, there is still a market today, mainly in cosmetics and pharmaceuticals.

Shark-liver oil pills were once an important source of vitamin A, creating a high market value for sharks during the 1940s and '50s. Deep-sea sharks were particularly targeted, as their livers can measure 20 percent of their body weight and contain up to 90 percent squalene oil. After the discovery of a synthetic source of the vitamin, the demand dropped sharply, but there is a continued market for the oil, which is used in products such as Preparation H, a hemorrhoid ointment with international distribution.

Shark-Fin Soup

Shark-fin soup is a highly regarded delicacy in Chinese culture, with a long history that dates back to the Ming Dynasty. Today the dish is traditionally served at weddings, banquets and corporate events. A rise in demand for this luxury dish has followed upon increasing economic prosperity, now that more people can afford the cost (up to US$100 per bowl). The fin cartilage itself provides no real taste, mainly texture, and is known to contain elevated amounts of toxic mercury. Still, the soup is considered highly prestigious and is culturally important to those who consume it.

The price of a shark's fins exceeds the monetary value of the rest of its body by up to a hundred times. This high demand has promoted the practice of "finning," in which only the fins are retained and the rest of the shark's body is discarded at sea. Up to 100 million sharks are finned each year for shark-fin soup, and often the shark is finned alive — the equivalent of cutting off a human's arms and legs and leaving him to die.

Millions of sharks are killed annually for their fins, which are used in the traditional Chinese delicacy shark-fin soup. However, shark-fin soup may pose a risk not just for sharks but for its consumers as well. Sharks are extremely high in mercury. Animals cannot naturally detoxify from mercury contamination, and since sharks are at the top of the food chain, they accumulate the mercury ingested by prey items all the way down to the bottom of the chain. In addition to mercury, recent research has demonstrated that shark fins contain high levels of a neurotoxin that has been linked to neurodegenerative diseases, including Alzheimer's disease and ALS.

Shark-finning is a brutal and wasteful practice. The shark's entire body is worth far less than its fins, and it weighs considerably more. A fishing vessel loaded to capacity will carry a much more valuable haul if only the fins are retained. Fins also do not require ice, a further burden; instead they can be dried and stowed away.

A bowl of shark-fin soup fetches a lofty price and signals high status at the weddings and business events where it is served. The literal translation from Mandarin is "fish-fin soup," which can be confusing for consumers who have perhaps heard that sharks are imperiled but do not make that connection to the dish.

Shark fins drying on a rack look very similar, but some belong to endangered species. A number of shark species are already endangered worldwide and protected under CITES, the Convention on International Trade in Endangered Species of Wild Fauna and Flora. Internationally protected species include the great white, basking, whale, scalloped hammerhead, smooth hammerhead, great hammerhead, oceanic whitetip, porbeagle and sawsharks. However, once the fins are removed from the body, identifying what species they come from is very difficult. New genetic techniques are now able to accurately identify not only what species of shark a fin comes from but also in what region that shark was caught. These analyses have already helped document illegal trade in great white shark fins, indicating that stronger measures are needed to enforce protection of species identified as endangered.

Sharkskin

In its raw or untanned state, known as shagreen, a shark's skin retains the minute sharp dermal denticles that give it its tough, abrasive quality. Shagreen was once used for sanding and polishing wood in the arts and crafts, and also as a striking surface for matches; another use was for sword hilts and body armor. Today's manufactured products have largely made the use of shagreen obsolete.

Sharkskin can be also be tanned to produce high-quality leather for luxury handbags, boots, belts, book bindings and furniture. During the tanning process the dermal denticles are removed; the end product is a smooth and very tough leather. A decreasing portion of leather production today is from sharks; however, they continue to be a valuable source of exotic leather.

Cartilage

In the twenty years since the claim was first made that shark cartilage may provide a cure for cancer, clinical trials have failed to produce supporting evidence. The idea began with initial observations that some concentrated extracts of cartilage could inhibit tumor formation. The link was made to sharks via a false assertion by I. William Lane, in a book titled *Sharks Don't Get Cancer* in 1992. The book received broad publicity, including a spot on the television program *60 Minutes*, and the concept captured the imagination of millions of hopeful cancer patients and medical practitioners.

But sharks do get cancer. Evidence of cancer in sharks in fact dates back to 1907, and numerous cases of both benign and malignant tumors in sharks have been clearly documented in scientific registries. There is still hope that highly purified components of cartilage might someday be successfully applied to fighting cancer. As with numerous pharmaceutical findings from nature, however, once a truly effective extract is isolated, it can often be manufactured synthetically, avoiding endangerment of species.

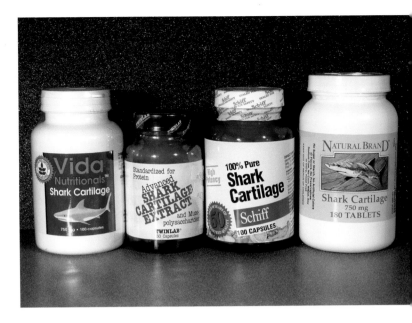

ABOVE: Shark cartilage products can be found on the shelves of any pharmacy or natural foods store. The market for shark cartilage has increased substantially over the past decade, and it maintains a high price. Some of the major producing and consuming nations are the United States, Japan, Australia and India. Shark cartilage can be found in powder, capsule or tablet form and is taken for numerous ailments ranging from acne to hemorrhoids, but principally for preventing and treating cancer. A major concern is that sharks continue to be killed for their cartilage even though there is no scientific evidence for its effectiveness.

LEFT: Sharkskin cowboy boots peaked in popularity during the 1980s but are still manufactured today in Texas and Mexico. The leather is durable and exotic. Interestingly, fishermen have to choose on the boat whether their catch will be sold for skin or for meat, since each requires very different treatment and processing. Shark meat is transported and sold with the skin intact to protect the flesh and avoid oxidation, but exposure to the fresh water from ice damages the skin. On the other hand, if not bled, dressed and iced soon after capture, the meat will spoil.

Hunting the Newborns

Many shark species travel to shallow coastal areas, known as shark nurseries, to have their pups. The pups school together in these sheltered waters until they have grown enough to move out into the adult habitat. As catches have dwindled over the past few decades, shark fishermen have increasingly had to target baby sharks to support their trade. Juvenile sharks are collectively called *cazón* in Mexico, and they are hunted in the shallow coastal nursery areas where they naturally gather, making them easy to find every year following pupping season. In a survey of small-scale fisheries in the upper Sea of Cortez, at least 14 of 17 species of sharks captured there were regularly taken as newborns or juveniles. Similar fishing efforts directed at juvenile sharks are reported farther south, throughout Central and South America. Taking too many young sharks at an early age, before they have had a chance to reproduce, can be detrimental to shark populations.

A catch of baby sharks is sorted and cleaned on a beach on the Sea of Cortez, Baja, Mexico. A local market for baby shark meat, called *cazón*, provides an incentive to target sharks before they have had a chance to reproduce. The Sea of Cortez is a productive inland sea and important nursery area for a large variety of shark species. Shark nurseries are generally in shallow coastal areas and are therefore highly accessible to local fishing communities. Fishermen who know that the sharks gather there every year in concentrated numbers don't always understand the implications of harvesting newborns before the sharks have a chance to reproduce and sustain their population.

Fear and Fascination

Ancient Demons

Sharks were deeply entwined in the spiritual lives of many early human cultures, particularly in regions such as the tropical Pacific and Latin America. In many of those societies a fundamental connection was felt between people and sharks. Among Australian Aboriginals, some clans of the Yolngu people claim descent from a mythical shark known as Mäna. In the Solomon Islands and in Hawaii it was believed that certain ancestors had been reincarnated as sharks. In these cultures sharks were worshiped; as deities they could bring good or bad fortune to their devotees.

In early European cultures, sharks were mostly perceived as evil, and some of the earliest records of sharks depict their attacks on humans. Greek and Roman images of sharks resembled sea monsters or serpents; a *ketos* was a sharklike creature described in ancient Greece as a monster of never-abating gluttony that ravened for food in a continual frenzy. The Greek philosopher Aristotle made important early scientific observations of sharks, distinguishing them from other fish by their cartilaginous skeleton, and referred to them as *selache*. The Romans dubbed sharks "dog-fish" or "sea fox" (*volpes marina*). Interestingly, references to sharks largely disappeared from European historical accounts throughout the Middle Ages, and only resurfaced when European sea exploration took off during the 16th century.

Sharks in Popular Culture

Sharks have always been revered and feared in our collective psyche. However, the mythology of sharks took an unfortunate turn in 1974–75, with the release of the book and subsequent movie *Jaws*. Author Peter Benchley's portrayal of white sharks as relentless, vicious killers was exquisitely fleshed out by director Steven Spielberg, and *Jaws* became the benchmark narrative of sharks in the modern world. Countless Hollywood productions have built on this same theme, essentially demonizing sharks for generations.

Peter Benchley's ability to craft a compelling narrative came from his deep experiential knowledge of the ocean. Seeing how profoundly his message had affected society, he spent the rest of his life trying to undo those negative perceptions and fighting to raise awareness of the plight of sharks, with comparatively limited success. In 2002 he published *Shark Trouble: True Stories about Sharks and the Sea*, a collection of nonfiction stories and discussions of shark behavior and conservation, pointing out how rare shark attacks really are. The book sold modestly, and today a hardcover edition can be purchased for less than a dollar. By contrast, the book *Jaws* has sold more than 20 million copies.

"Bruce," the animatronic white shark created for the film *Jaws*, measured 7.6 meters (25 feet) long and its jaws spanned 1.5 meters (5 feet). The largest reliable measurement for a real white shark (*Carcharodon carcharias*) is 6 meters (19.7 feet). There were in fact three models made, all the same size and all named Bruce, after director Steven Spielberg's lawyer, Bruce Ramer. Although technicians struggled on set to get Bruce to operate properly, the final product onscreen succeeded in scaring millions, typecasting sharks as cold, vindictive killers for generations to come.

Shark Tourism

While the future of some shark species looks grim, entrepreneurs in coastal areas, as well as local governments, are starting to figure out that sharks may be worth more alive than dead. Increasing numbers of people want to encounter sharks in their natural environment and are willing to spend a lot of money to get up close with these toothy ocean-dwellers. Shark tourism has been around for many decades. Adventurous divers were entering shark cages to observe and photograph great white sharks in Australia, feeding grey reef sharks in the Maldives and watching Caribbean reef sharks off the Bahamas back in the early 1980s, but the popularity of "shark diving" has really taken off in the past 15 years. It is this relatively new recreational activity that may help save sharks.

How widespread is shark tourism? In 2010 nearly 400 ecotourism operators in 29 different countries were promoting opportunities to swim with sharks, and this number continues to grow rapidly with the recognition that this can be a very lucrative industry. Which species are the most popular to seek out? It turns out that the whale shark is targeted by more operators than any other, namely in the Caribbean, the Philippines, Australia, the Seychelles and the Maldives. Whale sharks congregate at specific sites in response to predictable availability of a food source. For example, off Western Australia hundreds of whale sharks (mainly immature males) show up in autumn during coral and fish spawns, which attract the crustacean plankton the sharks eat. In the Caribbean these behemoths gather in the spring to feed on eggs produced by spawning assemblages of snappers.

The second most popular group of sharks sought out at dive sites around the world is the requiem sharks (family Carcharhinidae): Caribbean reef, bull, common blacktip, blacktip reef, grey reef, lemon and tiger sharks. In some locations requiem sharks can be predictably found at certain dive spots where they aggregate during the day, but they often don't hang around when divers appear on the scene. For this reason many dive operators use bait — this is known as provisioning — to ensure that their guests can get close to the sharks they have paid to see. This feeding of sharks has created much controversy (more on this later).

Shark diving generates millions of dollars a year for many local island and coastal economies. Worldwide it is estimated that whale-shark viewing alone generated more than US$47.5 million in 2004, while a small industry providing opportunities to snorkel with tiger sharks off South Africa generated US$1.8 million in 2007. Off the island of Moorea, in French Polynesia, a population of sicklefin lemon sharks generates US$5.4 million a year; by one calculation,

each resident shark contributes an average of US$474,000 per annum to the local economy, and up to US$2.64 million during its lifetime.

How does all this ecotourism benefit sharks? The monetary value of the live animals may encourage local people and their governments to make sure their local shark populations stay happy and healthy. For example, when a group of grey reef sharks was wiped out at a dive site in the Maldives, the Ministry of Fisheries and Agriculture banned all types of shark fishing within the main tourism zone. Why? Because it was estimated that the loss of revenue caused by extermination of the sharks at that one dive site came to about US$500,000 per year.

Even more extensive legislation was enacted in the Philippines after feeding groups of whale sharks were "discovered" off the small fishing village of Donsol. Groups of whale sharks predictably aggregate to feed on plankton in this area between November and June, and locals had begun offering tourists the opportunity to swim with these sharks. After rogue fishermen killed seven of these

While it was once the sport of a wealthy, elite few, now seeing a white shark in the wild is an experience had by a large number of scuba divers. White shark tourism now thrives off South Africa, South Australia and Baja, California.

Whale shark tourism has blown-up in tropical seas around the world. These massive sharks, and adventuresome snorkelers looking for a thrilling experience, help support local economies located where whale sharks form predictable feeding aggregations. Some governments are protecting these sharks in coastal waters, at least in part for the financial benefits they provide. Here are group of snorkelers observe a whale shark off the coast of Western Australia.

animals, the Philippines government declared the area a whale-shark sanctuary in 1998. Subsequently hunting and trading in whale sharks was banned throughout the Philippines because of the potential revenue shark viewing could generate for the country. Ask the people living along the coastline adjacent to Ningaloo Reef, Western Australia, how big whale-shark ecotourism can get. Since 1989, swimming with these ocean giants has been big business. Whale-shark tourism there is calculated to generate from US$2.5 million to around $4.8 million per annum for the local economy.

As mentioned earlier, the most controversial issue in shark diving involves provisioning. First of all, there is the potential danger it may pose to humans. It has been suggested that sharks may begin to associate people (and boats) with

Welcome to the shark circus! A group of neophyte shark-watchers form a semi-circle around a feeding station, complete with a chain-mail-clad shark wrangler and well-mannered Caribbean reef sharks. In the end, it may be our fascination with sharks that helps keep at least some shark populations from being decimated.

food, which could increase the likelihood of their approaching and behaving aggressively toward divers. It has also been suggested that "collateral damage" may occur to locals who have nothing to do with the shark industry but swim or dive in the area where these conditioned sharks occur. Abalone divers in South Australia have expressed concern that chumming white sharks exposes the divers to greater danger because there are more sharks in the area as a result of the shark-diving industry and the sharks learn to associate boats with food. Likewise, in South Africa swimmers and surfers have expressed concern over chumming activities being carried out adjacent to public beaches.

People participating in shark feeds have been bitten. Between 1979 and 2001, 47 percent of shark bites that occurred in French Polynesia took place

Divers' fascination with and desire to see large sharks in their natural habitat may help save them from extinction. Shark ecotourism can encourage local governments to protect their shark populations. It also gives people an opportunity to experience and observe these amazing animals in situ, which in turn stimulates a desire to save them. While there may be some downside to feeding sharks, it is greatly outweighed by the conservation efforts that may result from shark tourism. Here a well-mannered Fijian bull shark accepts an offering from its greatest nemesis, a human.

during dives where bait was present, although none of these were fatal injuries. In most cases the people bitten are dive operators distributing food to the sharks, but that is not always the case. One of the few fatal attacks at a shark feed occurred in the Bahamas, when a tourist diver was bitten on the calf by a bull shark.

Another possible downside of provisioning is the negative impact it could have on the sharks themselves. If a shark is regularly getting a free handout at a dive site, it may hang around the area and reduce its natural home range. This could lead to more inbreeding and a reduction in genetic exchange, which could cause long-term harm to the population. This possibility has been suggested for a group of sicklefin lemon sharks that visit feeding sites off the island of Moorea. Shark feeding can also increase the number of interactions between non-gregarious shark species. This may increase the number of aggressive encounters between sharks, elevate stress levels and lead to increased transmission of ectoparasites.

Some shark species may alter their activity patterns or habitat usage as a result of provisioning. On Osprey Reef, in the Coral Sea, whitetip reef sharks are normally active at night, moving up and down the reef in search of food, while during the day they are mostly inactive, spending much of their time in repose on deeper sand flats at the base of the reef — that is, except on the days when dive boats are present and food is provisioned during shark dives. During those periods the whitetips are much more active during the day and spend more time at shallower depths, where they interact with both the divers and other sharks (mainly grey reef sharks). This has the potential to adversely affect the whitetips' energy budget and their overall fitness. As it turns out, the whitetips get very little to eat during these feeds, as most of the rations are consumed by the more dominant grey reef sharks. Fortunately, because of its remoteness, few dive boats get to Osprey Reef and the sharks infrequently experience the effects of provisioning.

The same cannot be said about the Stingray City sandbars off Grand Cayman Island in the Caribbean. Here is an elasmobranch population that has been greatly impacted by human activity. Since 1984 tourist boats have been pulling up to this location from early morning to mid-afternoon as snorkelers and divers feed bits of squid to more than 100 southern stingrays (*Dasyatis americana*). The site has become so popular that as many as 2,500 tourists on 40 tour boats may visit the site simultaneously. The behavior of this population of stingrays has changed drastically. These animals, which are normally nighttime hunters, have become diurnal. While they are typically solitary animals, here they engage in group living. Their home ranges have been greatly reduced, and as a result this location has become a mating as well as a feeding site. *Dasyatis* at Stingray City have more external parasites and more wounds, the result of aggressive interactions between individuals and from boat propellers and predators.

Fortunately, in most cases research has indicated that food provisioning at dive sites has relatively little impact on large shark species. Studies conducted at a site where Caribbean reef sharks have been fed for more than 20 years indicated no apparent behavioral shift in the population; that is, when it came to their residency or movements in a particular area, the individuals that participated in shark feeds behaved no differently than sharks that did not. The same conclusion was drawn in a study conducted on tiger sharks that visited "Shark Beach" in the Bahamas. Having access to provisioning had no impact on long-distance migration and habitat use in these large tigers.

Can Sharks Survive?

For perhaps the first time in their illustrious 400 million years of success, sharks are now in danger. Humans have taken the place of Earth's top predator, and our powerful reach extends into every corner of the oceans. While scientists have suspected for a long time that sharks may be in trouble from overfishing, it has been only in the past five to ten years that a systematic evaluation of sharks' conservation status has been undertaken, a task carried out by the International Union for Conservation of Nature (IUCN). Nearly half of sharks, especially deep-sea species, still cannot be assessed because there are insufficient data on catch rates and population numbers. However, as of 2009, 32 percent of open-ocean sharks (for example, blue, mako and oceanic whitetip sharks) were classified as threatened — 6 percent as endangered and 26 percent as vulnerable to extinction. For 25 percent of these species, data were lacking with which to evaluate them.

Unlike lions and tigers and other land-based predators that are threatened by loss of habitat, the major threat to sharks can be directly attributed to overfishing. The reason sharks are so vulnerable is their slow growth and low reproductive rate. Their population numbers simply cannot increase fast enough to compensate for the losses. If the 420 million years of shark evolutionary history were the equivalent of a single summer of growth and success, the present threat to sharks would have occurred only in the last 1.36 seconds. In the course of their entire history, it is likely that sharks have never encountered a greater threat. Their fate truly lies in our hands.

Whether the sharks are the target or simply unintentional bycatch, their fins are most frequently sliced off as they are being pulled aboard. The practice of shark-finning has been banned by an increasing number of countries, but enforcement on the high seas is difficult, and the motivation for illegal fishing and trafficking is high, given the fins' market value. An additional step has been to ban the sale or transport of shark fins altogether. This policy action has been adopted by a number of governments by popular vote. Within the United States, trade in shark fins has been banned in all Pacific Rim states, including Hawaii, Alaska, Washington, Oregon and California.

References

Aalbers, S.A., D. Bernal D. and C.A. Sepulveda. "The Functional Role of the Caudal Fin in the Feeding Ecology of the Common Thresher Shark *Alopias vulpinus*." *Journal of Fisheries Biology* 76 (2010): 1863–68.

Abel, R.L., J.S. Maclaine, R. Cotton, V.B. Xuan, T.B. Nickels, T.H. Clark, Z. Wang and J.P.L. Cox. "Functional Morphology of the Nasal Region of a Hammerhead Shark." *Comparative Biochemistry and Physiology Part A: Molecular and Integrative Physiology* 155, no. 4 (2010): 464–75.

Barnett, A., K.G. Abrantes, J.D. Stevens, B.D. Bruce and J.M. Semmens. "Fine-Scale Movements of the Broadnose Sevengill Shark and Its Main Prey, the Gummy Shark." *PLoS ONE* 5, no. 12 (2010): e15464.

Barnett, A., J.M. Braccini, C.A. Awruch and D.A. Ebert. "An Overview on the Role of Hexanchiformes in Marine Ecosystems: Biology, Ecology and Conservation Status of a Primitive Order of Modern Sharks." *Journal of Fish Biology* 80, no. 5 (2012): 966–90.

Benchley, P. *Jaws*. New York: Doubleday Books, 1974.

———. *Shark Trouble: True Stories about Sharks and the Sea*. New York: Random House, 2002.

Bigelow, H.B., and W.G. Schroeder. *Fishes of the Gulf of Maine*. Fishery Bulletin of the Fish and Wildlife Service 53. Washington, DC: US Department of the Interior, 1953.

Camhi, M.D., S.V. Valenti, S.V. Fordham, S.L. Fowler and C. Gibson. *The Conservation Status of Pelagic Sharks and Rays: Report of the IUCN Shark Specialist Group Pelagic Shark Red List Workshop*. Newbury, UK: IUCN Species Survival Commission Shark Specialist Group, 2009.

Carey, F.G., J.M. Teal and J.W. Kanwisher. "The Visceral Temperatures of Mackerel Sharks (Lamnidae)." *Physical Zoology* 54, no. 3 (1981): 334–44.

Cartamil, D.P., C.A. Sepulveda, N.C. Wegner, S.A. Aalbers, A. Baquero and J.B. Graham. "Archival Tagging of Subadult and Adult Common Thresher Sharks (*Alopias vulpinus*) off the Coast of Southern California." *Marine Biology* 158, no. 4 (2011): 935–44.

Claes, J.M., and J. Mallefet. "Functional Physiology of Lantern Shark (*Etmopterus spinax*) Luminescent Pattern: Differential Hormonal Regulation of Luminous Zones." *Journal of Experimental Biology* 213, no. 11 (2010): 1852–58.

Clua, E., N. Buray, P. Legendre, J. Mourier and S. Planes. "Behavioural Response of Sicklefin Lemon Sharks *Negaprion acutidens* to Underwater Feeding for Ecotourism Purposes." *Marine Ecology Progress Series* 414 (2010): 257–66.

———. "Business Partner or Simple Catch? The Economic Value of the Sicklefin Lemon Shark in French Polynesia." *Marine and Freshwater Research* 62, no. 6 (2011): 764–70.

Compagno, L.J. *FAO Species Catalog*. Vol. 4, *Sharks of the World: An Annotated and Illustrated Catalog of Shark Species Known to Date*. Part 1, *Hexanchiformes to Lamniformes*. Part 2, *Carchariniformes*. Fisheries Synopsis 125. Rome: Food and Agriculture Organization, 1984.

Cortés, E. "Life History Patterns and Correlations in Sharks." *Reviews in Fisheries Science* 8, no. 4 (2000): 299–344.

Cox, J.P.L. "Hydrodynamic Aspects of Fish Olfaction." *Journal of the Royal Society Interface* 5, no. 23 (2008): 575–93.

Cressey, R.F., and E.A. Lachner. "The Parasitic Copepod Diet and Life History of Diskfishes (Echeneidae)." *Copeia* (1970): 310–18.

Dawson, C.L., and R.M. Starr. "Movements of Subadult Prickly Sharks *Echinorhinus cookei* in the Monterey Canyon." *Marine Ecology Progress Series* 386 (2009): 253–62.

Daly-Engel, T.S., R.D. Grubbs, K.N. Holland, R.J. Toonen and B.W. Bowen. "Assessment of Multiple Paternity in Single Litters from Three Species of Carcharhinid Sharks in Hawaii." *Environmental Biology of Fishes* 76, no. 2 (2006): 419–24.

Deecke, V.B., J.K.B. Ford and P.J.B. Slater. "The Vocal Behaviour of Mammal-Eating Killer Whales: Communicating with Costly Calls." *Animal Behaviour* 69, no. 2 (February 2005): 395–405, doi:10.1016/j.anbehav.2004.04.014.

Dowd, W.W., G.M.C. Renshaw, J.J. Cech and D. Kultz. "Compensatory Proteome Adjustments Imply Tissue-Specific Structural and Metabolic Reorganization Following Episodic Hypoxia or Anoxia in the Epaulette Shark (*Hemiscyllium ocellatum*)." *Physiological Genomics* 42, no. 1 (2010): 93–114.

Dulvy, N.K., J.K. Baum, S. Clarke, L.J.V. Compagno, E. Cortés, A. Domingo, S. Fordham, S. Fowler, M.P. Francis, C. Gibson, J. Martínez, J.A. Musick, A. Soldo, J.D. Stevens and S. Valenti "You Can Swim but You Can't Hide: The Global Status and Conservation of Oceanic Pelagic Sharks and Rays." *Aquatic Conservation: Marine and Freshwater Ecosystems* 18, no. 5 (2008): 459–82.

Dulvy, N.K., and J.D. Reynolds. "Evolutionary Transitions among Egg-Laying, Live-Bearing and Maternal Inputs in Sharks and Rays." *Proceedings of the Royal Society of London*, ser. B, 264, no. 1386 (1997): 1309–15.

Ebert, D.A., and L.J. Compagno. "*Chlamydoselachus africana*, a New Species of Frilled Shark from Southern Africa (Chondrichthyes, Hexanchiformes, Chlamydoselachidae)." *Zootaxa* 2173 (2009): 1–18.

Fergusson, I.K., K.J. Graham and L.J. Compagno. "Distribution, Abundance and Biology of the Smalltooth Sandtiger Shark *Odontaspis ferox* (Risso, 1810) (Lamniformes: Odontaspididae)." *Environmental Biology of Fishes* 81, no. 2 (2008): 207–28.

Fish, F.E., and L.D. Shannahan. "The Role of the Pectoral Fins in Body Trim of Sharks." *Journal of Fish Biology* 56, no. 5 (2000): 1062–73.

Fitzpatrick, R., K.G. Abrantes, J. Seymour and A. Barnett. "Variation in Depth of Whitetip Reef Sharks: Does Provisioning Ecotourism Change Their Behaviour?" *Coral Reefs* 30, no. 3 (2011): 569–77.

Forey, P., and P. Janvier. "Agnathans and the Origin of Jawed Vertebrates." *Nature* 361 (January 1993): 129–34, doi: 10.1038/36112a0.

Gallagher, A.J., and N. Hammerschlag. "Global Shark Currency: The Distribution, Frequency, and Economic Value of Shark Ecotourism." *Current Issues in Tourism* 14, no. 8 (2011): 797–812.

García, V.B., L.O. Lucifora and R.A. Myers. "The Importance of Habitat and Life History to Extinction Risk in Sharks, Skates, Rays and Chimaeras." *Proceedings of the Royal Society*, ser. B., 275, no. 1630 (2008): 83–89.

Gardiner, J.M., and J. Atema. "The Function of Bilateral Odor Arrival Time Differences in Olfactory Orientation of Sharks." *Current Biology* 20, no. 13 (2010): 1187–91.

Gemballa, S., P. Konstantinidis, J.M. Donley, C. Sepulveda and R.E. Shadwick. "Evolution of High-Performance Swimming in Sharks: Transformations of the Musculotendinous System from Subcarangiform to Thunniform Swimmers." *Journal of Morphology* 267, no. 4 (2006): 477–93.

Gilmore, G.R., J.W. Dodrill and P.A. Linley. "Reproduction and Embryonic Development of the Sand Tiger Shark, *Odontaspis taurus* (Rafinesque)." *Fishery Bulletin* 81, no. 2 (1983): 201–25.

Gleiss, A.C., S.J. Jorgensen, N. Liebsch, J.E. Sala, B. Norman, G.C. Hays, F. Quintana et al. "Convergent Evolution in Locomotory Patterns of Flying and Swimming Animals." *Nature Communications* 2 (2011): 352, doi:10.1038/ncomms1350.

Graham, R.T., C.M. Roberts and J.C. Smart. "Diving Behaviour of Whale Sharks in Relation to a Predictable Food Pulse." *Journal of the Royal Society Interface* 3, no. 6 (2006): 109–16.

Gruber, S.H., and J.L. Cohen. "Visual System of the White Shark, *Carcharodon carcharias*, with Emphasis on Retinal Structure." *Memoirs of the Southern California Academy of Sciences* 9 (1985): 61–72.

Guttridge, T.L., S.H. Gruber, K.S. Gledhill, D.P. Croft, D.W. Sims and J. Krause. "Social Preferences of Juvenile Lemon Sharks, *Negaprion Brevirostris*." *Animal Behaviour* 78, no. 2 (2009): 543–48.

Hammerschlag, N., A.J. Gallagher, J. Wester, J. Luo and J.S. Ault. "Don't Bite the Hand That Feeds: Assessing Ecological Impacts of Provisioning Ecotourism on an Apex Marine Predator." *Functional Ecology* 26, no. 3 (June 2012): 567–76.

Hazin, F., and R. Lessa. "Synopsis of Biological Information Available on Blue Shark, *Prionace glauca*, from the Southwestern Atlantic Ocean." *Collective Volume of Scientific Papers* (ICCAT) 58, no. 3 (2005): 1179–87.

Heithaus, M., A. Frid and L. Dill. "Shark-Inflicted Injury Frequencies, Escape Ability, and Habitat Use of Green and Loggerhead Turtles." *Marine Biology* 140, no. 2 (2002): 229–36.

Heupel, M.R., and C.A. Simpfendorfer. "Quantitative Analysis of Aggregation Behavior in Juvenile Blacktip Sharks." *Marine Biology* 147, no. 5 (2005): 1239–49.

Holland, K.N., B.M. Wetherbee, C.G. Lowe and C.G. Meyer. "Movements of Tiger Sharks (*Galeocerdo cuvier*) in Coastal Hawaiian Waters." *Marine Biology* 134, no. 4 (1999): 665–73.

Hueter, R.E., M.R. Heupel, E.J. Heist and D.B. Keeney. "Evidence of Philopatry in Sharks and Implications for the Management of Shark Fisheries." *Journal of Northwest Atlantic Fishery Science* 37 (2004): 239–47.

Hutchings, J.A. "Life Histories of Fish." In *Handbook of Fish Biology and Fisheries,* Vol. 1, *Fish Biology*, edited by P.J.B. Hart and J.D. Reynolds, 149–74. Oxford: Blackwell Science, 2003.

Huveneers, C., R.G. Harcourt and N.M. Otway. "Observation of Localised Movements and Residence Times of the Wobbegong Shark *Orectolobus halei* at Fish Rock, NSW, Australia." *Cybium* 30, no. 4 (2006): 103–11.

Jorgensen, S.J., N.S. Arnoldi, E.E. Estess, T.K. Chapple, M. Rückert, S.D. Anderson and B.A. Block. "Eating or Meeting? Cluster Analysis Reveals Intricacies of White Shark (*Carcharodon carcharias*) Migration and Offshore Behavior." *PLoS ONE* 7, no. 10 (October 29, 2012): e47819, doi:10.1371/journal.pone.0047819.

Jorgensen, S.J., A.P. Klimley and A.F. Muhlia-Melo. "Scalloped Hammerhead Shark, *Sphyrna lewini*, Utilizes Deep-Water, Hypoxic Zone in the Gulf of California." *Journal of Fish Biology* 74, no. 7 (2009): 1682–87.

Jorgensen, S.J., C.A. Reeb, T.K. Chapple, S. Anderson, C. Perle, S.R. Van Sommeran, C. Fritz-Cope, A.C. Brown, A.P. Klimley and B.A. Block. "Philopatry and Migration of Pacific White Sharks." *Proceedings of the Royal Society*, ser. B, 277 (2010): 679–88.

Kajiura, S.M. "Head Morphology and Electrosensory Pore Distribution of Carcharhinid and Sphyrnid Sharks." *Environmental Biology of Fishes* 61, no. 2 (2001): 125–33.

Kalmijn, A. "Electric and Magnetic Field Detection in Elasmobranch Fishes." *Science* 218, no. 4575 (1982): 916–18.

Keeney, D.B., M.R. Heupel, R.E. Hueter and E.J. Heist. "Microsatellite and Mitochondrial DNA Analyses of the Genetic Structure of Blacktip Shark (*Carcharhinus limbatus*) Nurseries in the Northwestern Atlantic, Gulf of Mexico, and Caribbean Sea." *Molecular Ecology* 14, no. 7 (2005): 1911–23, doi:10.1111/j.1365-294X.2005.02549.x.

Keyes, R.S. "Sharks: An Unusual Example of Cleaning Symbiosis." *Copeia* 1982, no. 1 (1982): 225–27.

Klimley, A.P. "The Determinants of Sexual Segregation in the Scalloped Hammerhead Shark, *Sphyrna lewini*." *Environmental Biology of Fishes* 18, no. 1 (1987): 27–40.

———. "Highly Directional Swimming by Scalloped Hammerhead Sharks, *Sphyrna lewini*, and Subsurface Irradiance, Temperature, Bathymetry and Geomagnetic Field." *Marine Biology* 117, no. 1 (1993): 1–22.

Klimley, A.P., S.C. Beavers, T.H. Curtis and S.J. Jorgensen. "Movements and Swimming Behavior of Three Species of Sharks in La Jolla Canyon, California." *Environmental Biology of Fishes* 63, no. 2 (2002): 117–35.

Klimley, A.P., and D.R. Nelson. "Diel Movement Patterns of the Scalloped Hammerhead Shark (*Sphyrna lewini*) in Relation to El Bajo Espiritu Santo: A Refuging Central-Position Social System." *Behavioral Ecology and Sociobiology* 15, no. 1 (1984): 45–54.

Kröger, B., T. Servais and Y. Zhang. "The Origin and Initial Rise of Pelagic Cephalopods in the Ordovician." *PLoS ONE* 4, no. 9 (2009): e7262, doi:10.1371/journal.pone.0007262.

Kyne, P.M., L.J.V. Compagno, J. Stead, M.V. Jackson and M.B. Bennett. "Distribution, Habitat and Biology of a Rare and Threatened Eastern Australian Endemic Shark: Colclough's Shark, *Brachaelurus colcloughi* Ogilby, 1908." *Marine and Freshwater Research* 62, no. 6 (2011): 540.

Kyne, P.M., and C. Simpfendorfer. "Deepwater Chondrichthyans." In *Sharks and Their Relatives*. Vol. 2, *Biodiversity, Adaptive Physiology and Conservation*, edited by J.C. Carrier, J.A. Musick and M.R. Heithaus, 37–114. Boca Raton, FL: CRC Press, 2010. http://www.crcnetbase.com/doi/pdf/10.1201/9781420080483-c2.

Lane, I.W., and L. Comac. *Sharks Don't Get Cancer*. Avery, 1992.

Lineaweaver, T.H., and R.H. Backus. *The Natural History of Sharks*. London: Andre Deutsch, 1970. http://www.getcited.org/pub/101607592.

Lingham-Soliar, T. "Dorsal Fin in the White Shark, *Carcharodon carcharias*: A Dynamic Stabilizer for Fast Swimming." *Journal of Morphology* 263, no. 1 (2005): 1–11.

Lund, R., and E. Grogan. "The Origin and Relationships of Early Chondrichthyes." In *Biology of Sharks and Their Relatives*, edited by J. Musick, J. Carrier and M. Heithaus, 3–31. Boca Raton, FL: CRC Press, 2004. http://www.crcnetbase.com/doi/pdf/10.1201/9780203491317.pt1.

MacArthur, R.H., and E.O. Wilson. *The Theory of Island Biogeography*. Princeton, NJ: Princeton University Press, 1967.

Magnuson, J.J., and R.M. Gooding. "Color Patterns of Pilotfish (*Naucrates ductor*) and Their Possible Significance." *Copeia* 1971, no. 2 (1971): 314–16.

Meredith, T.L., and S.M. Kajiura. "Olfactory Morphology and Physiology of Elasmobranchs." *Journal of Experimental Biology* 213, no. 20 (2010): 3449.

Michael, S.W. "Reef Sharks and Rays of the World: A Guide to Their Identification, Behavior and Ecology." Monterey, CA: Sea Challengers, 1993.

Motta, P.J., M. Maslanka, Robert E. Hueter, R.L. Davis, R. de la Parra, S.L. Mulvany, M.L. Habegger, J.A. Strother, K.R. Mara, J.M. Gardiner, J.P. Tyminski and L.D. Zeigler. "Feeding Anatomy, Filter-Feeding Rate and Diet of Whale Sharks *Rhincodon typus* during Surface Ram Filter Feeding off the Yucatan Peninsula, Mexico." *Zoology* 113, no. 4 (2010): 199–212.

Mull, C.G., K.E. Yopak and N.K. Dulvy. "Does More Maternal Investment Mean a Larger Brain? Evolutionary Relationships between Reproductive Mode and Brain Size in Chondrichthyans." *Marine and Freshwater Research* 62, no. 6 (2011): 567–75.

Myrberg, A.A. "The Acoustical Biology of Elasmobranchs." *Environmental Biology of Fishes* 60, no. 1 (2001): 31–46.

Nakamura, I., Y.Y. Watanabe, Y. P. Papastamatiou, K. Sato and C.G. Meyer. "Yo-yo Vertical Movements Suggest a Foraging Strategy for Tiger Sharks *Galeocerdo cuvier*." *Marine Ecology Progress Series* 424 (2011): 237–46.

Naylor, Gavin JP, Janine N. Caira, Kirsten Jensen, Kerri AM Rosana, Nicolas Straube, Clemens Lakner, J. Carrier, J. Musack, and E. Heithaus. "Elasmobranch Phylogeny: A Mitochondrial Estimate Based on 595 Species." In *The Biology of Sharks and Their Relatives*, 31–57. edited by J. C. Carrier, J. A. Musick, and M. R. Heithaus. CRC Press, 2012.

Nelson, D.R., J.N. McKibben, W.R. Strong, C.G. Lowe, J.A. Sisneros, D.M. Schroeder and R.J. Lavenberg. "An Acoustic Tracking of a Megamouth Shark, *Megachasma pelagios*: A Crepuscular Vertical Migrator." *Environmental Biology of Fishes* 49, no. 4 (1997): 389–99.

Oliver, S., N. Hussey, J. Turner, and A. Beckett. "Oceanic Sharks Clean at Coastal Seamount." *PloS ONE* 6, no. 3 (2011): e14755.

Ostrander, G.K., K.C. Cheng, J.C. Wolf and M.J. Wolfe. "Shark Cartilage, Cancer and the Growing Threat of Pseudoscience." *Cancer Research* 64, no. 23 (2004): 8485–91.

Papastamatiou, Y.P., B.M. Wetherbee, J. O'Sullivan, G.D. Goodmanlowe and C.G. Lowe. "Foraging Ecology of Cookiecutter Sharks (*Isistius brasiliensis*) on Pelagic Fishes in Hawaii, Inferred from Prey Bite Wounds." *Environmental Biology of Fishes* 88, no. 4 (2010): 361–68.

Pillans, R.D., J.D. Stevens, P.M. Kyne and J. Salini. "Observations on the Distribution, Biology, Short-Term Movements and Habitat Requirements of River Sharks *Glyphis* spp. in Northern Australia." *Endangered Species Research* 10 (2009): 321–32.

Prince, E., and C. Goodyear. "Hypoxia-Based Habitat Compression of Tropical Pelagic Fishes." *Fisheries Oceanography* 15, no. 6 (2006): 451–64.

Queiroz, N., N.E. Humphries, L.R. Noble, A.M. Santos and D.W. Sims. "Short-Term Movements and Diving Behaviour of Satellite-Tracked Blue Sharks *Prionace glauca* in the Northeastern Atlantic Ocean." *Marine Ecology Progress Series* 406 (2010): 265–79.

Skomal, G.B., and G.W. Benz. "Ultrasonic Tracking of Greenland Sharks, *Somniosus microcephalus*, under Arctic Ice." *Marine Biology* 145, no. 3 (2004): 489–98. http://www.springerlink.com/content/cu8fpf31a22mbj43/.

Smale, M.J., W.H. Sauer and R.T. Hanlon. "Attempted Ambush Predation on Spawning Squids *Loligo vulgaris reynaudii* by Benthic Pyjama Sharks, *Poroderma africanum*, off South Africa." *Journal of the Marine Biological Association of the United Kingdom* 75 (1995): 739–42.

Smith, K., M. Scarr and C. Scarpaci. "Grey Nurse Shark (*Carcharias taurus*) Diving Tourism: Tourist Compliance and Shark Behaviour at Fish Rock, Australia." *Environmental Management* 46, no. 5 (2010): 699–710.

Sneader, W. *Drug Discovery: A History*. Chichester, UK: John Wiley and Sons, 2005.

Stevens, J.D., R.W. Bradford and G.J. West. "Satellite Tagging of Blue Sharks (*Prionace glauca*) and Other Pelagic Sharks off Eastern Australia: Depth Behaviour, Temperature Experience and Movements." *Marine Biology* 157, no. 3 (2010): 575–91.

Strasburg, D.W. "The Diet and Dentition of *Isistius brasiliensis*, with Remarks on Tooth Replacement in Other Sharks." *Copeia* 1963, no. 1 (1963): 33–40.

Sundstrøm, L.F., S.H. Gruber, S. M. Clermont, J.P. Correia, J. R. de Marignac, J. F. Morrissey, C.R. Lowrance. L. Thomassen and M.T. Oliveira. "Review of Elasmobranch Behavioral Studies Using Ultrasonic Telemetry with Special Reference to the Lemon Shark, *Negaprion brevirostris*, around Bimini Islands, Bahamas." *Environmental Biology of Fishes* 60, no. 1 (2001): 225–50.

Tanaka, S., Y. Shiobara, S. Hioki, H. Abe, G. Nishi, K. Yano and K. Suzuki. "The Reproductive Biology of the Frilled Shark, *Chlamydoselachus anguineus*, from Suruga Bay, Japan." *Japanese Journal of Ichthyology* 37, no. 3 (1990): 273–91.

Tricas, T.C. "Bioelectric-Mediated Predation by Swell Sharks, *Cephaloscyllium ventriosum*." *Copeia* (1982): 948–52.

Vianna, G.M.S., M.G. Meekan, D.J. Pannell, S.P. Marsh and J.J. Meeuwig. "Socioeconomic Value and Community Benefits from Shark-Diving tourism in Palau: A Sustainable Use of Reef Shark Populations." *Biological Conservation* 145, no. 1 (January 2011): 264–77.

Visser, I. "Benthic Foraging on Stingrays by Killer Whales (*Orcinus orca*) in New Zealand Waters." *Marine Mammal Science* 15, no. 1 (1999): 220–27.

Ward-Paige, C.A., D.M. Keith, B. Worm and H.K. Lotze. "Recovery Potential and Conservation Options for Elasmobranchs." *Journal of Fish Biology* 80, no. 5 (2012): 1844–69, doi:10.1111/j.1095-8649.2012.03246.x.

Wetherbee, B.M., and E. Cortés. "Food Consumption and Feeding Habits." In *Biology of Sharks and Their Relatives*, edited by J. Musick, J. Carrier and M. Heithaus, 223–42. Boca Raton, FL: CRC Press, 2004.

Widder, E.A. "A Predatory Use of Counterillumination by the Squaloid Shark, *Isistius brasiliensis*." *Environmental Biology of Fishes* 53, no. 3 (1998): 267–73.

Wueringer, B.E., L. Squire and S.P. Collin. "The Biology of Extinct and Extant Sawfish (Batoidea: Sclerorhynchidae and Pristidae)." *Reviews in Fish Biology and Fisheries* 19, no. 4 (2009): 445–64.

Index

Photo credits

Jim Abernethy / Seapics.com: 210–211. Kelvin Aitken / MarineThemes.com: 12 top left; 12 top center; 13 top; 26–27; 28; 29; 32; 34; 36; 39 top; 59; 71; 92–93; 98–99; 143 left center; 143 bottom right; 199. Julie Anderson / SharkAngels.com: 222 bottom left; 225. Scot Anderson: 138. Jason Arnold: 44 inset. Michael Aw: 66–67. Fred Bavendam / Minden Pictures: 157 top; 209. George W. Benz / SeaPics.com: 70. Jonathan Bird / Seapics.com: 102–103; 109. Sam Cahir / Seapics.com: 104–105. Nick Caloyianis / National Geographic Image Collection: 111. Dr. Steven Campana, Bedford Institute of Oceanography, Canada: 134. Mark Carwardine / OceanwideImages. com: 154. Brandon Cole: 2; 19; 23; 24–25; 78–79; 80 bottom left; 88; 95 top; 106; 114 bottom left; 116–117; 143 top right; 147; 149 left; 155; 156–157 bottom right; 169; 183; 207 top; 213; 219; 222 bottom right; 239; 244. Phillip Colla / OceanLight.com; 212. Mark Conlin / Seapics.com: 13 bottom; 75; 95 bottom. Bob Cranston / SeaPics.com: 133 left center. Wayne Davis: 113 left. Reinhard Dirscherl / SeaPics.com: 171. David Doubilet / National Geographic Image Collection: 114 bottom right; 143 top second from left; 222 top right; 229. Chris and Monique Fallows / Apex Predators: Inside cover; 115 top; 161; 194; 195; 214; 216–217. Chris and Monique Fallows / OceanwideImages.com: 41; 136–137; 163. David Fleetham / OceanwideImages.com: 82; 144; 149 right. Jurgen Freund / NPL / Minden Pictures: 143 top left; 156 bottom left; 204–205. Louis Goldman, NBC / Universal: 241. Florian Graner / NPL / Minden Pictures: 58. Tom Haight / SeaPics.com: 57. Dave Harasti: 80 top right; 110. Jeffrey Hartog: 159. Adrian Hepworth / NHPA / Photoshot: 74. Richard Herrmann: 69, 185. Hirose / e-Photography / SeaPics.com: 223 top; 232–233. Alex Hyde / NPL / Minden Pictures; 121 bottom left; 121 bottom right. Image Quest Marine: 133 top left. Stephen Kajiura: 51. Marilyn and Maris Kazmers, Sharksong Photography: 237. David Kearnes / SeaPics.com: 176–177. Avi Klapfer / Seapics: 172–178. Yasumasa Kobayashi / Nature Production / Minden Pictures: 81 top; 87. Hans Leijnse / Foto Natura / Minden Pictures: 65. Gwen Lowe / SeaPics.com: 196. Oliver Lucanus / Foto Natura / Minden Pictures: 64. Prof Jérôme Mallefet, research associate FNRS at UCL: all photos on 130–131. Scott Michael: 39 bottom; 113 right; 114 top right; 124 top; 124 bottom; 125 top; 125 bottom; 126 top; 126 bottom; 127; 128 top; 128 bottom; 129 top; 129 bottom; 137; 202–203; 205 (inset). Albert LLeal Moya / Minden Pictures: 114 top left; 121 top left; 121 top right. Andy Murch / Elasmodiver: 12 bottom right; 15; 33; 35; 37; 68; 112; 187; 188–189; 207 bottom. Andy Murch / MarineThemes.com: 48–49, 133 center right. Andy Murch / OceanwideImages.com: 42–43; 156 top right; 175 top. Museum of New Zealand Te Papa Tongarewa: 146 (inset). Chris Newbert / Minden Pictures: 7. Flip Nicklin / Minden Pictures: 143 center second from left; 200–201. OceanLab: 90–91. Michael Patrick O'Neill / SeaPics.com: 243. Pete Oxford / Minden Pictures: 16–17. Doug Perrine / NPL / Minden Pictures: 61; 81 bottom; 89; 132–133; 133 bottom right; 150–151; 235. Doug Perrine / SeaPics.com: 72–73; 100–101; 139; 156 top left; 167; 208; 235. Chris Rainier/Corbis: 161. Jeff Rotman: 45–46; 80 top left; 83; 223 bottom; 245. Jeff Rotman / NPL / Minden Pictures: 119; 123; 143 top second from right; 143 center second from right; 143 center right; 143 bottom left; 143 bottom second from left; 143 bottom second from right. Jeff Rotman / SeaPics.com: 222 top left; 230. Nuno Sá: 4–5; 115 bottom; 140; 152–153; 190–191; 192–193. Andy Sallmon: 64. D. R. Schrichte / SeaPics.com: 133 bottom right. Brian Skerry / National Geographic Image Collection: 31; 180–181. Marty Snyderman / SeaPics.com: 170. Rob Stewart / Sharkwater: 231. Mark Strickland / Seapics.com: 249. Valerie Taylor / Ardea: 107. Masa Ushioda / SeaPics.com: 197; 220–221. James D. Watt / Seapics.com: 47; 175 bottom. Randy Wilder / Monterey Bay Aquarium: 12 bottom left; 77. Jeff Wildermuth: 145. Steve Williams: 84–85. D. P. Wilson / FLPA / Minden Pictures: 80 bottom right; 96–97 all; 120. Jim Wilson / The New York Times / Redux: 230 top left. Associate Professor Stephen Wroe, University of Newcastle, Australia: 135. Norbert Wu / Minden Pictures: 133 top right; 178–179; 226–227.

Cover: © DLILLC / Corbis
Back cover: © Chris and Monique Fallows / OceanwideImages.com

Acknowledgments:

I would like the thank the following friends and colleagues for their invaluable contributions. Dr. Cheryl A. Logan provided thoughtful and constructive feedback on the concepts, content and writing. Drs. Adrian C. Gleiss and Gavin J. P. Naylor provided scientific figures from their recent research. Drs. Wesley W. Dowd, Danna J. Staaf and Taylor K. Chapple provided feedback on concepts and scientific accuracy. Their patient and generous help made this book possible.

Additional contributions:

Aaron B. Carlisle, PhD – Subject consultation, research and editing
Kristin B. Ingram – Photo research and acquisition